Think Through
Geography 1

Mike Hillary
Julie Mickleburgh
Jeff Stanfield

Longman

Edinburgh Gate
Harlow, Essex

Contents

Contents

1 What is Geography?

Introduction

A stormy coastline in Dingle, Ireland

A busy street in Shanghai, China

People and place

Geography is all around us. Geographers investigate places, and look at what gives places their character. One place may be very different from another place. The character of a place depends on its physical and human features, and on the people who live there.

Geographical features can be **human** or **physical**.

Physical features are natural things in the landscape, like hills, rivers and the weather.

Human features are made by people – things like towns and cities that are made up of houses, factories, shops, roads and railways.

You often hear about physical features when they hit the news headlines, e.g. a volcanic eruption, an earthquake or a flood.

Increasingly, human features affect our environment, for example, the effects of pollution on the atmosphere, or of changes in farming methods on our food supply.

People, patterns and processes

In geography you will study how physical and human features are created and changed by geographical **processes**. One example of a physical process is erosion, which slowly wears away the land. An example of a human process is migration – the movement of people from one place to another.

Geographical **patterns** are made when human and physical features form shapes or arrangements that are repeated in different places. For example, streets and houses are sometimes arranged in similar patterns in towns and cities across the world. Rivers and coastlines also form patterns which can be seen in different parts of the world.

1 a What geographical *features* can you see in the photographs on pages 4 and 5?
  b Which are *physical* and which are *human* features?
2 Spend a few minutes looking at the photographs in this book. Make a list of five *physical features* and five *human features* that you can see, for example:

Physical features	Human features
cliffs	buildings

Homework
- Collect some pictures of human and physical features. Use them to cover your book, or to make a class display.
- Add labels and captions to your pictures, indicating whether they are physical or human features.

A volcano erupting

The Lake District, Cumbria

People and the environment

Geographers investigate the connections between people and their environment – how people affect the environment and how the environment affects people's lives. To do this they may look at many different topics, which could range from litter around a school to global warming of the planet!

Each of the enquiries in this book is divided into three sections:

- People and Place.
- People, Patterns and Processes.
- People and Environment.

YOUR ENQUIRY

In the following enquiry you will study a place. You will:
- use key geographical questions to find out about the character of a place and how it is changing
- use a range of geographical skills in order to answer the key questions
- evaluate the usefulness of resources.

At the end of the enquiry you will look at the similarities and differences between your local area – 'Our local area' – and Banjul, a city in West Africa.

http://www.bbc.co.uk/education-webguide/pkg_main.p_home
(Search for geography.)

1a What is Geography?

• How can places be investigated? •

In geography we can use key questions to find out about a place. In this book you will be investigating the world around you in a series of enquiries.

This enquiry is about a place. You need to become a *place detective*! A detective is someone who asks questions in order to gather evidence. To do that you need to know what questions geographers ask when they investigate a place.

Here is a picture of a place called Banjul.

| 1 What is it? | 2 Where is it? | 3 What is it like? | 4 How did it get like this? |

A

| 5 How is it changing? | 6 Why is it changing? | 7 What might happen in the future? |

How much can you find out about the place just by looking at one photograph, using key geographical questions? We will be using these key questions to investigate places throughout this book.

- What other questions might you ask to find out more about this place?
- What things can we **not** tell from a photograph?

1 What is it?

Banjul is a capital city. It is the capital of The Gambia. The Gambia is a small country in West Africa.

2 Where is it?

Banjul is on the Atlantic coast, at the western end of the country and on the western edge of Africa. It is situated on a narrow strip of land called a **peninsula**, which juts out into the **estuary** of the River Gambia.

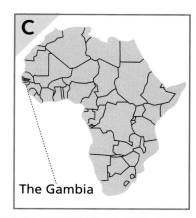

C

The Gambia

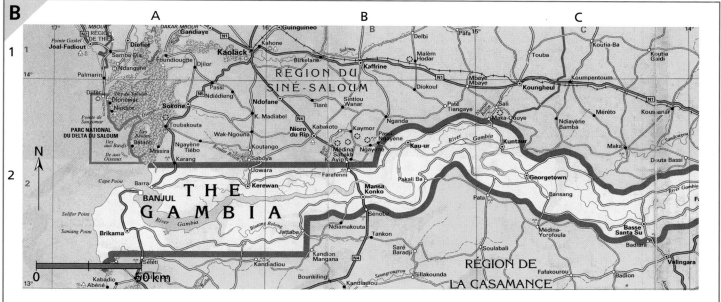

The Gambia. Reproduced from the 1996 Macmillan Education Ltd map of The Gambia

D Latitude and longitude

We can identify the location of a place using latitude and longitude. These are imaginary lines, used on a map to locate places. Lines of latitude and longitude are measured in degrees.

The lines of latitude are horizontal lines on a map and are labelled in degrees north and south of the Equator (0°).

Lines of longitude are vertical lines on a map and are labelled in degrees east and west of the Greenwich Meridian (0°).

STEP 1

1 a Find Banjul in map **B** above.
  b What is the latitude and longitude of Banjul?
2 a In which *part* of the country is Banjul – north, south, east or west?
  b Use an atlas to name some of the countries next to the Gambia.
3 How big is The Gambia compared with other countries in Africa?

http://www.netline.be/gambia/index

3 What is it like?

As the country's major port, Banjul exports most of The Gambia's main crop, which is groundnuts (we sometimes call them peanuts). It is a busy city with wide roads and modern buildings in the centre. Surrounding the city centre are large areas of single-storey houses made out of concrete blocks and tin roofs where most of the people live (see photograph **A** on page 6). There are schools, shops, offices and street markets selling fruit, vegetables, fish and meat.

Banjul is The Gambia's main centre for business, government and education.

A

Wellington Street

B

Russell Street

C

Picton Street

D | **The Gambia** | **Banjul**

Banjul is a dusty place, but safe. A visit to Albert Market, where plenty of good-natured bargaining goes on to get the best price, is a must. There is a tourist market nearby where you can buy local crafts and jewellery. The shops in Russell Street, Nelson Mandela Street and Wellington Street have a stunning range of fabrics, and there are plenty of local tailors who will make clothes for you. Remains of the colonial past include the State House and MacCarthy Square, where the game of cricket is still played. Places of interest include the Great Mosque, the Catholic Cathedral and St Mary's Anglican Cathedral.

A traveller's guide

STEP 2

How much more can we find out about Banjul from photographs? Look at photographs **A**, **B** and **C** and photograph **A** on page 6. Consider these questions:

- What type of place is it? Is it small or large? Is it busy or quiet?
- What types of buildings does it have?
- What are the streets like?
- Is it a village, a town or a city?
- What sorts of clothes are the people wearing?
- What jobs do you think people do?
- What would it be like to live in Banjul?
- What does the guide tell us that we cannot tell from photographs?

4 How did it get like this?

When geographers ask this question, they have to look into the past to find out how a place has changed. They may use old maps and history books to find out what happened. Geographers want to find out what changes have taken place – and *why*. If the place is a town or a city then we need to know the reasons for its location, and why it grew there.

Look for Independence Drive in grid squares C1, C2 and D2 on map **E**. This street name gives us a clue about the history of the country. The Gambia was a British **colony** from 1821 until it became an independent country in 1970. In that time Banjul grew from a small settlement on what was then an island in the River Gambia, to a city of more than 60,000 people. The main reason for its growth has been that Banjul is a port and trading centre on the western edge of Africa. Crops that are grown inland (mostly groundnuts and cotton) are sent through Banjul to other parts of the world, especially to countries in Europe.

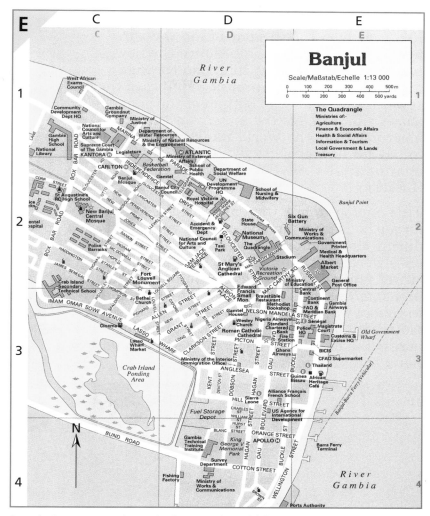

Banjul. Reproduced from the 1996 Macmillan Education Ltd map

Banjul is the capital city of The Gambia. The street plan of Banjul gives us another clue to the history of the city. The British laid out the streets in straight lines, in a style that is known as a 'grid pattern'.

STEP 3

Look carefully at map **E**.

1 In which grid squares are the Central Mosque, the Anglican Cathedral and the Roman Catholic Cathedral?
2 Name three places of interest in D2.
3 Where are most of the government offices and buildings in Banjul?
4 Draw a sketch map of part of Banjul to show the pattern of streets in the city.

5 State two pieces of evidence on the map showing that Banjul is a *capital* city.

Homework/Extension

You are staying at the Atlantic Hotel in D1. Plan a walk that takes in six of the main sites and places of interest.

5 How is it changing?

Photograph **A** shows some of the ways in which Banjul is changing. Notice the new pavement that is being laid, and the sign about the new drains project to improve the sewerage system. The bottom of the sign shows that some of the money for the project has come from the World Bank, which helps to pay for new projects like this in less economically developed countries (LEDCs).

This photograph **A** was taken in 1997. The larger houses in the photograph were built during the colonial period and the smaller ones were built later, by the local people. Water pipes and taps have been put into some areas and people can now go to a nearby tap to collect water. Notice the telephone and electricity lines, which are also spreading across the city. Some shops now sell second-hand fridges and freezers.

Photograph **B** shows the corner of Picton Street and Wellington Street (see map **E** on page 9). Here the large supermarket sells the same type of goods that you would expect to find in a British supermarket. Although not everyone in Banjul can afford them, more and more modern goods and clothes are appearing in the shops.

Until they were paved, the alleyways in photograph **C** were just earth ditches, and many had sewage running down them, which often brought disease.

6 Why is it changing?

As people living Banjul earn more money so they want a better standard of living. The demand for services such as water, electricity and sanitation has grown. When there is a regular electricity supply people begin to buy electrical goods.

7 What might happen in the future?

With improvements in housing, roads and services, cities in the LEDCs are beginning to look more and more like towns and cities in the UK. As life in the cities improves for some people, even more people try to move into the city in search of work and a better life.

STEP 4

1 Look closely at the photographs on pages 6–10. In your own words, describe some of the recent changes in Banjul.
2 Suggest what may happen in the future as a result of these changes.

• photograph interpretation • using key questions •

THINKING THROUGH YOUR ENQUIRY

In this enquiry you have investigated one place, Banjul. You are now ready to be a place detective. Your task is to investigate a place that you know well – your local town or city – and then compare it with Banjul. Use the key geographical questions to organise your research.

'Our local area'

1 What is it?

- A village, a town, a suburb, a city borough, an industrial town, a market town, a regional centre, a port, a holiday area …?

2 Where is it?

- Describe its location (latitude and longitude) using an atlas.
- If possible, use an Ordnance Survey map and give a four-figure grid reference.
- Is it north, south, east or west of other places?
- Is it on a hill, by the coast or on a river?
- Draw a labelled sketch map to show the location of the place you have chosen.

3 What is it like?

- Describe the landscape – physical and human features.
- What is the character of the place (busy/quiet, large/small)?
- Briefly describe the industries (jobs), transport (road and rail), people.

4 How did it get like this?

- What is the history of your local area?
- What changes took place?
- What were the reasons for its growth?

5 How is it changing?

- What are the recent changes – new houses? industries?

6 Why is it changing?

- People moving in or moving out?
- Fewer jobs? New jobs?

7 What might happen in the future?

Extension

What other questions might you ask about your local area? For example:

- How is it linked to other places – in the UK or the world?
- How is it affected by other places and by decisions made elsewhere?
- How has its importance changed over time?

Answer these questions, and then compare your local area with Banjul using a table like this:

	Local town or city	Banjul
What is it?	. . . .	. . . .
Where is it?	. . . .	. . . .
What is it like?	. . . .	. . . .
How did it get like this?	. . . .	. . . .
How is it changing?	. . . .	. . . .
Why is it changing?	. . . .	. . . .
What might happen in the future?	. . . .	. . . .

Homework

Choose another town or city somewhere else in the world and compare it with your local area, e.g. Cherbourg (page 84) or Nairobi (page 108).

What resources can we use?

To find out what a place is like we can either visit the place or look at pictures and photographs. Television, video, CD-ROMs, magazines, newspapers, books and the Internet can all provide words and pictures to describe what a place is like.

You need to decide what resource to use when researching a place.

• What are patterns and processes? •

• Where can we see patterns?

Have you ever noticed how some things – like houses in a street, or pebbles on a beach – are arranged in certain ways? These arrangements are called **patterns**. Geographers try to *describe* the **patterns** using resources like maps and aerial photographs. They then try

• How do we describe processes?

to *explain* how and why these patterns have been created. In order to do this they need to understand the physical and human **processes** that are at work creating these patterns.

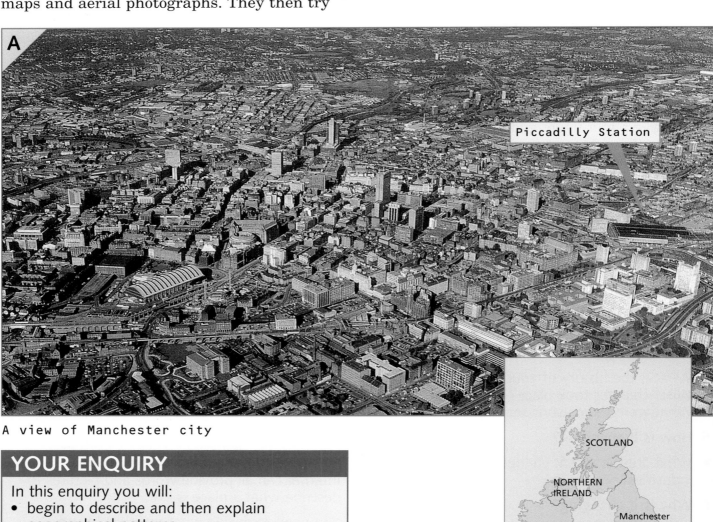

A view of Manchester city

Piccadilly Station

Where is Manchester?

YOUR ENQUIRY

In this enquiry you will:
• begin to describe and then explain geographical patterns
• begin to explain geographical processes.

At the end of the enquiry you will investigate 'Patterns and processes in your local area'.

Human patterns

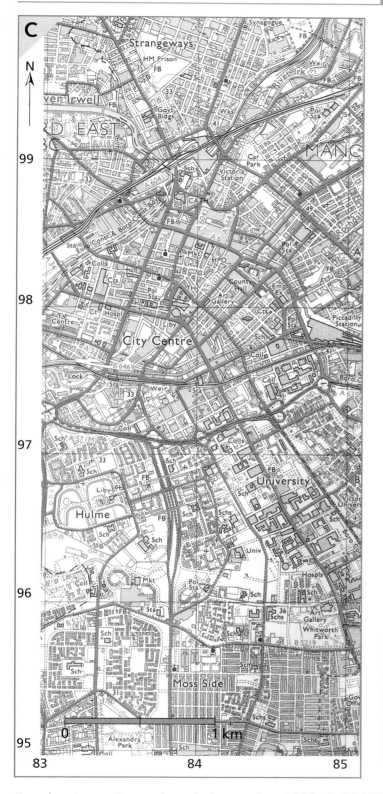

C

Human patterns are created by people, and are the result of people's activities. The street patterns in different parts of Manchester are an example of human patterns. They are the result of several periods of development in the past. The straight rows of terraced houses date back to the Victorian period, when Manchester was a rapidly growing industrial city. Many of these houses were built for people who worked in the cotton and textile factories. In those days working people did not have cars, and they had to walk to work. There were no garages or gardens. Houses had backyards and there were alleyways running between the rows of houses.

In the period between the two World Wars, especially during the 1930s, new houses were built on new streets with curved or even circular patterns, next to the older Victorian streets.

In the 1960s, some areas of old terraced housing in the city were knocked down and new blocks of flats were built in their place.

More recently, housing estates have been built further out from the city centre. These estates often have curved or crescent-shaped street patterns.

STEP 1

1 Find the city centre in grid squares (GR) 8397, 8398, 8497 and 8498 on map **C**. Name three important buildings labelled in the city centre.
2 Look at photograph **A** and name three different types of land use you can see.
3 How do you know this photograph contains the city centre.
4 Compare the pattern of roads in the city centre with those in GR8495.
5 What is the pattern of land use in GR8496?

Manchester. Reproduced from the 1982 1:25000 Ordnance Survey map of Manchester and Ashton-Under-Lyne by permission of the Controller of HMSO © Crown copyright

 http://www.bbc.co.uk/education/mapping

 • using number co-ordinates •

Physical patterns

Physical features such as hills, valleys, volcanoes and rivers form physical patterns. We can also study the physical patterns of rainfall and temperature created by the processes of weather and climate. The maps below show patterns of rainfall and relief. Relief is the word used to describe the height and slope of the land.

Map **A** shows the relief of the British Isles.

Map **B** shows the pattern of rainfall across the British Isles during an average year. The key shows the total number of millimetres of rainfall for each year.

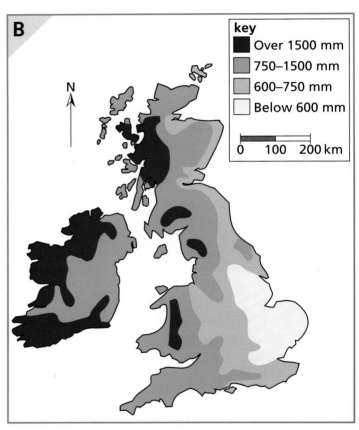

A

key
- Over 400 m
- 100–400 m
- Below 100 m

N

0   100   200 km

Relief map of the British Isles

B

key
- Over 1500 mm
- 750–1500 mm
- 600–750 mm
- Below 600 mm

N

0   100   200 km

Rainfall across the British Isles

STEP 2

1 a Look carefully at map **A**. Using an atlas, name *two* areas of high land.

   b What do you notice about the pattern of high land in the British Isles? Which parts of the country are the highest – the north and west, or the south and east?

2 a Look at map **B**. Which parts of the British Isles have the highest rainfall – the north and west, or the south and east?

   b Describe the **pattern** of rainfall across the British Isles.

3 Compare the patterns of relief and rainfall. Use the following words in your answer:
- north
- south
- east
- west
- coast
- inland.

Extension

Try to explain the pattern of rainfall. You could use pages 53–54 to help.

Physical processes

Processes are going on all around us, all of the time. Some of the processes **erode** away the land (see photograph **C**).

Other processes **transport** material like sand and shingle along a beach.

The process of **deposition** creates new land when material is deposited in a different location like a sand *spit* or river *delta*.

Rivers wear away the land by the process of erosion

STEP 3

1 Use a dictionary to find out the exact meaning of the following words:
   • erosion • deposition • transportation • weathering.
   Write down the dictionary definitions in your notebook.
2 Copy diagram **E** below. Add the following labels in the correct boxes.
   • weathering • transport • deposition • erosion • evaporation • condensation.
3 Name two ways in which material can be transported after it has been eroded.
4 **a** Where does weathering, e.g. peeling paint, crumbling bricks or concrete, weathered tiles, slates or flat roofs, take place around your school?
   b Can you observe and name any areas of your school grounds which are being eroded by the feet of people moving around the school?

The outside of this school building is crumbling away by the process of weathering

Extension

Mark on a plan of your school grounds the areas where the buildings are being weathered and the ground is being eroded.
How are the weathered areas linked to the weather and how are areas of erosion linked to the movement of people around the school?

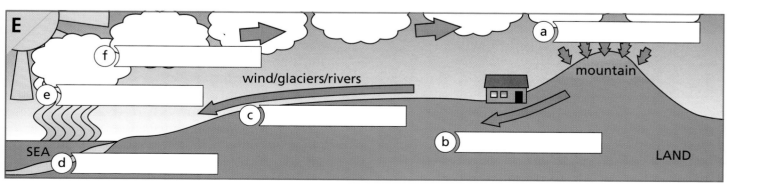

Human processes

People change the world around them. These changes are called human processes.

More and more people now live in towns and cities. All over the world towns have grown larger and larger over the years. This process is called **urbanisation** (photograph **A**).

In some towns and cities, old buildings are being knocked down and new buildings put up in their place. This process is called **redevelopment** (photograph **B**).

Human processes also include the movement of people around the world. The movement of people is called **migration**. When people move out of a country it is called emigration. When people move into a country, it is called immigration. Some movements are semi-permanent when people move to find work within the same continent, like the many Turkish people who have moved to Germany to find jobs. Other people move permanently, for example in the 1950s many West Indian people were encouraged to move to the UK to find work. Some migrations are seasonal, for example when people move to harvest crops in another area.

Many migrants move to find better jobs or improved living conditions, but some are *forced* to move because of war, natural disaster or religious and ethnic troubles, such as the people of Kosovo in 1999.

B

Redevelopment in Docklands, London

C

Refugees leave Zaire for Rwanda

A

Urbanisation in Eccles, Manchester

STEP 4

1 What processes can you see in photographs **A**, **B** and **C**?
2 Look around your local area. Describe any places where new housing is being built, or where there is redevelopment. What is happening? How is it affecting the people who live there?
3 Do you know of anyone arriving in or leaving the country to work or live in another country? Or anyone who has moved in the past?
   Either find out how they felt, *or* imagine you are leaving the country to work abroad. What would you have to leave behind? What would you look forward to? How would you feel about the move?

THINKING THROUGH YOUR ENQUIRY

How does a geographer find out about patterns and processes? Your task is to carry out a geographical investigation into patterns and processes in your local area, or in a place nearby.

'Patterns and processes in our local area'

1 Ask a key geographical question.

You could choose one of the following key questions or make up your own:
- What is the most important type of land use in the local area?
- How is the land use changing?
- Where are the busiest roads?
- How are any new developments affecting different groups of people?

You might need to break these down into smaller questions, e.g. land use – What is the landscape like? What buildings are there? How are the roads arranged – in straight rows or in curves (crescents)?

2 Decide what information you need to collect.

- You might go out into the local area observing and recording information, e.g. land use – marking on a map what buildings are used for in different streets.
- You might count cars and vehicles as they pass along a road to find out where the busiest roads are.
- You might ask people for their views on any recent changes.

3 Collect and record information.

You will need to decide on the best ways to collect data. You might:
- use a map
- create a table of results
- use a spreadsheet or a database to store and retrieve information.

4 Present the data and information collected.

You need to show what you have found out, by drawing maps and graphs. You can use graph paper, Ordnance Survey maps or the computer.

5 Describe and explain your enquiry.

- What was the question?
- What did you do to find answers to your question?
- Describe the process of collecting and recording data.
- Describe and explain your findings/results.
- What do the maps and graphs tell you about any patterns and processes in the local area?

6 Draw conclusions.

- Have you answered the original question? If not, why not?
- What problems did you have?

7 Finally ...

- Are there any ways in which you could have improved your enquiry?
- Are there any further questions you could investigate in your local area?

Extension

Using e-mail, exchange information about your area with another school using the same questions.

1c What is Geography?

• What are environmental issues? •

- What is the environment?
- Why is it important to all of us?
- Why do different people have different opinions about the environment?
- How do we change the environment?

The environment is made up of the natural environment and the human environment. The natural and human parts of the environment are connected in many different ways. If we damage one part of the environment other parts can be affected as well. Some environmental issues are right on our doorstep and for some people, like those in newspaper articles **A** and **B**, these issues are worth protesting about.

A

Judge allows eco-warrior, 11, to carry on living in protesters' tree house

AN 11-YEAR-OLD boy known as General Survival was given permission by the High Court yesterday to remain in his tree house home.

Matthew Williams was not allowed to speak in the case because of his age, but fellow eco-warriors spoke on his behalf at the hearing before Mr Justice Astill.

Epsom and Ewell Borough Council in London had won a decision against the 20 protesters who moved into a park in the centre of Epsom after plans were agreed to fell trees for a road scheme.

Mr Justice Astill said they could appeal against the decision 'in the interests of justice' because it was possible that the eco-warriors had a case to argue.

Matthew said: 'It was really boring. I was not allowed to say anything. I wanted to tell him how much I love the green park and how much I want to save the silver birches.'

Matthew Williams in his tree-house home

Newspaper report, August 1998

YOUR ENQUIRY

In this enquiry you will:
- find out how to investigate an environmental issue
- begin to understand how people can improve and damage the environment
- learn why there are conflicting demands on the environment

- discover how people try to manage the environment
- find out what is meant by sustainable development.

At the end of the enquiry you will write a report on 'A local environmental issue'.

Everybody's environment

When some environmentalists heard of the plans to extend Manchester Airport by building a new runway, they decided to make a protest. There were a number of issues:

- local residents were concerned about the noise from the aircraft
- farmers were concerned about the loss of their farmland
- environmentalists were concerned about the destruction of the woodland wildlife habitat and the pollution of the nearby river Bodlin.

Manchester has the third busiest airport in the UK. Supporters of the second runway plan believed it was needed because:

- the first runway was busy at peak times, and could not handle all the air traffic
- more airlines wanted to use the airport
- many people now travelled from this area to Heathrow or Gatwick to transfer to an international flight – a new runway would allow more direct international flights
- it would attract new industry to the area, and provide jobs for people in the region.

B SAS-style raid on Swampy and pals

A dramatic dawn raid was launched yesterday to evict protesters at Manchester Airport.

Black-clad security men stormed the protestors' camp at the site of the £172 million second runway. They were followed in the 4 a.m. SAS-style operation by specialist tunnellers and climbers, backed up by police.

Tree dwellers – pals of eco-warrior Swampy* – hooted and whistled as their friends were dragged down, some in handcuffs, while others fled down tunnels.

Protesters branded the eviction squad 'heavy-handed bullies', amid claims that they lashed out with batons.

Joanna Lim, 21, from Manchester, said: 'Men with truncheons shouted for everyone to get on the ground and started kicking the men. It was terrifying.' But Cheshire Under-Sheriff Randal Hibbert, in charge of the massive operation, denied that anyone had weapons or attacked campaigners.

* 'Swampy' is the name of a man who tunnelled under the ground to protest against new roads and airports.

The protestors' camp at Manchester Airport

Newspaper report

STEP 1

1 Why did some people want the second runway at Manchester Airport?
2 Farmers and local residents, as well as environmentalists, were against the proposals. Can you think why?
3 Imagine you are a local resident living near the site of the new runway. Write a letter to the local newspaper, either for or against the proposed runway. Give three reasons why you think it is a good idea or a bad idea.

Extension

Re-read the newspaper item **A**. In what other ways can people protest against new road schemes? Find out some recent environmental issues where people are protesting.

---

 http://www.foe.org.uk

 • writing a persuasive letter • analysing a text •

Environmental pollution – everyone's responsibility?

'Environmental pollution' refers to all the ways that people can harm the natural environment. Most of us have seen environmental pollution in the form of a rubbish tip or a factory pouring out smoke. However, pollution can also be invisible, odourless and tasteless. For example, noise from traffic and machinery can be considered a form of pollution because it reduces people's quality of life.

Environmental pollution is one of the most serious problems facing people, animals and plants today. Badly polluted air can harm crops and cause life-threatening illnesses. Some air pollutants have reduced the ability of the atmosphere to filter out the sun's harmful rays, and many scientists believe that these and other air pollutants have begun to change climates around the world. Ocean pollution endangers many marine animals. Water and soil pollution threatens the ability of farmers to grow enough food to feed everyone.

A

Pollution from car exhaust

B

Oil-polluted beach

C

Canford Heath

One environmental issue can be seen at Canford Heath in Dorset. The heathland has been reduced to a few small areas. The plant and animal habitat is seriously threatened, and local campaigners have fought off threats from road- and house-building. Canford Heath is the home of a number of rare plants and animals, including the sand lizard, the smooth snake and the Dartford warbler. Fires,

D

GREENPEACE

How do people protect the environment?

E

In 1992 the United Nations organised the Rio Earth Summit in a response to the growing threat to the environment. At this conference, what may well be the most important document on Earth – Agenda 21 – was agreed upon and signed by all parties present. Agenda 21 is a programme designed to bring the planet back on a course towards sustainable development. Co-operation at local, national and international levels is sought, with partnerships between community and voluntary groups, businesses and local authorities.

No hope for heathland?

motorcycle-scrambling, rubbish tipping, and disturbance from people and dogs are all affecting the plants and animals. The site is a Site of Special Scientific Interest (SSSI), but the growth of the nearby town of Poole included plans to build new housing estates on Canford Heath, and a new road close to the edge of the heath.

To protect the heathland:

- campaigners tried to persuade the local council not to build more houses on the heathland
- the World Wide Fund for Nature and the society for lizards and snakes challenged the council's plans in court
- the local Friends of the Earth group teamed up with local residents to hold a public meeting and send out leaflets explaining why the scheme should not go ahead
- campaigners wrote and spoke to local councillors to try and convince them to abandon the scheme
- campaigners wrote to local newspapers.

Eventually the Departmentment of Transport moved the route to the very edge of Canford Heath.

F Protecting the environment

Local measures
- Bus lanes and traffic calming schemes are introduced in towns and cities to encourage people to use more public transport and to drive more carefully.
- In the countryside, country parks are set up to protect areas and to allow people to visit natural areas.
- Many councils have their own recycling schemes for rubbish and waste.

National measures
- Large areas of land are protected within national parks. In the UK, the USA and East Africa there are national parks in areas of outstanding natural beauty.
- In many countries there are national organisations like the National Trust, English Nature, the RSPB and the Woodland Trust, which all try to protect areas from further development.
- Groups such as Friends of the Earth try to prevent destruction of the environment and make people aware of the issues concerning the environment.

International measures
- International organisations like the World Wide Fund for Nature and Greenpeace campaign against the destruction of animals and the environment.
- The Convention on International Trade in Endangered Species (CITES) checks the sales of animals and birds.

STEP 2
1 Look at photographs **A** and **B**. Describe how people can damage the environment. Suggest what can be done to prevent this damage.
2 Look at the information on Canford Heath on pages 20–21. How was Canford Heath being damaged? Suggest what can be done to prevent further damage.

Homework/Extension
Work in groups, each group looking at one aspect of the environment, e.g. air, water and land. Research some of the ways in which the environment is being damaged. Each group should present their findings to the class. Finally, suggest ways of reducing environmental damage.

http://www.foe.co.uk/wildplaces
http://www.english-nature.org.uk

Sustainable development

The problem
As the number of people in the world increases, and as people want to improve their standard of living, the Earth's resources are put under more and more pressure. As we continue to use in great quantities resources like water, coal, oil, gas and minerals, these resources begin to run out. And as we extract raw materials, make things and transport them around the world, we also pollute the environment.

The solution
In order to prevent or reduce pollution and to conserve the Earth's resources, many people believe we need to work towards **sustainable development**. This means making things and using the environment in such a way that it is not destroyed for ever. It also means producing power and electricity from the wind (e.g. wind turbines), sun (e.g. solar panels) and water (e.g. hydro-electric turbines) instead of using up raw materials like coal, oil and gas.

A

Centre for Alternative Technology

The *Centre for Alternative Technology* in Mid-Wales demonstrates ways in which people, nature and technology can live together successfully. The natural world has many processes for survival. If we want to survive into the future our best bet lies with understanding and working with those processes, rather than trying to 'conquer' nature.

At the Centre you can see technologies and *ways of living* that do this, for example sewerage systems and generators that create power using sun, rain and wind.

Equally important are *ways of doing things*, for example composting in the garden, recycling bottles and cans in the home, turning off lights, using low-flush toilets, using bicycles instead of cars.

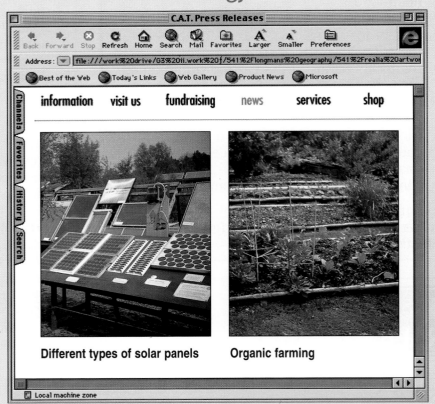

Different types of solar panels   Organic farming

STEP 3
1 Explain the term 'sustainable development'.
2 Suggest two ways of producing power without using up resources.
3 How do the people at the Centre for Alternative Technology try to live in a sustainable way?

Homework/Extension
Search the website for the Centre for Alternative Technology for other examples of sustainable development. (http://www.cat.org.uk).

THINKING THROUGH YOUR ENQUIRY

Geographers often investigate environmental issues. Are there any examples of environmental issues in your local area?

Such issues might involve:
- building new housing, or new roads
- conflict in a nearby national park or area of protected land, e.g. country park, SSSI, etc.
- new plans linked to transport or energy use.

3,000 new homes needed in ... by 2010

'A local environmental issue'

Your task is to write a report on a local environmental issue, and to give your own views. Use these key questions to help you.

Section 1
- What is the issue?
- What is it about?
- Where is it taking place? (Draw a map to show the location.)

Section 2
- Why is it happening?
- Who is involved? (Which groups of people?)

Section 3
- What views do these groups have about the issue? (Try to find quotes from people. Environmental groups often present information for their latest campaign over the Internet or on television and in the newspapers.)

Section 4
- Are there any alternative solutions or options to the problem you are studying?
- How can the issue be solved? What are *your* ideas?

Section 5
- Who will make the decision about the issue? How will it be made?
- What do *you* think? What are your feelings?
- What happened in the end? What was the outcome? *or* What do you think might happen?

Extension/Homework

Describe how you feel about one particular environmental issue, either national or international. Plan a letter to your local newspaper explaining what you think about the issue.

Continuing homework
- Collect information about environmental issues as they happen during your geography course.
- Collect information about one environmental organisation or one recent environmental issue. You could use the Internet sites given at the bottom of the page or contact the local environmental organisation on this page and pages 20–21.

 THE NATIONAL TRUST

http://www.cat.org.uk
http://www.wwf-uk.org
http://www.foe.co.uk/wildplaces

2a Settlement

• Can two cities be compared? •

London and Los Angeles: a tale of two cities

- What are your images of London and Los Angeles?
- How did these two cities develop?

Los Angeles and Hollywood

London and Oxford Street

The main activity of a settlement is described as its **function**. Settlements have different functions. They might be important industrial centres or shopping centres. They might be ports, capital cities or tourist centres. Large cities like London and Los Angeles have many different functions. The function of a settlement is often a connected to its location and growth.

YOUR ENQUIRY

In this enquiry you will:
- find out how London and Los Angeles are similar and how they are different
- discover the reasons for their location and growth
- learn about changes in the function of settlements
- explore some issues connected with urban areas.

At the end of the enquiry you will draw up 'A comparison between London and Los Angeles'.

Location and growth of Los Angeles

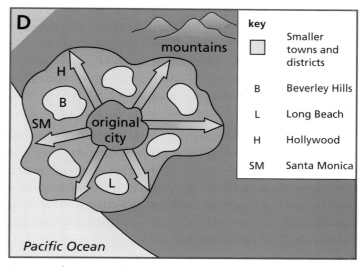

An agglomeration: growth of Los Angeles

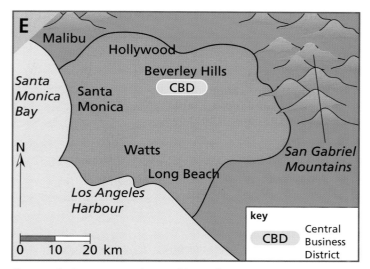

Map of Los Angeles district

Los Angeles is situated on the Pacific coast of California with mountains to the east and the north. In 1781 Los Angeles was a small community. It became a city in 1850 but did not begin to grow until the coming of the Southern Pacific railroad in 1875 and the Santa Fe railroad in 1885. Better communications enabled it to develop into a holiday resort and centre for orange growing. A harbour was built by 1914 and the port grew into the busiest on the Pacific coast of North America. The city's population had doubled by the 1920s due to the expanding oil industry and early film industry, centred in Hollywood. During and after the Second World War (1939–45) the area became a centre for aircraft manufacture.

Today Los Angeles is the second largest city in the USA, with over three and a half million people. It sprawls over 1,200 km² and has swallowed up surrounding areas, such as Beverly Hills and the San Fernando Valley. Geographers call this type of settlement an **agglomeration** (map **D**). Apart from the warm climate (good for farming) and being near the sea (good for communication), the main reason for the city's continued growth is the number of jobs available there. Los Angeles is now a major commercial, financial, computer and manufacturing centre.

STEP 1

1 Look at the photographs on page 24. What images do they give of London and Los Angeles?
2 Write a brief description of Los Angeles using the following sentences:
   • Los Angeles grew because …
   • Its major industries include …
   • It is called an agglomeration because …

http://www.city.netmaps
http://www.raingod.com/angus/Gallery/Photos/NorthAmerica

 • writing a description •

Location and growth of London

London is situated on the River Thames in the south-east of England. It grew as a port, trading with other countries. In the 18th and 19th centuries, when Britain had many colonies overseas, London imported food and resources from the colonies, and exported manufactured goods all over the world. Industries such as furniture and clothing developed along the river close to the docks, in areas like the East End.

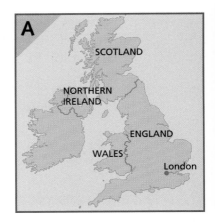

A

London has always been at the centre of transport routes. It continued to develop as a major industrial centre in the 19th century, as more industries grew along the canals and railways. In the 20th century most industrial development has been along the major roads. Today, with its major motorways and airports, London is an important route centre. The Channel Tunnel links the city by rail to all the major European centres.

Despite being a major centre for manufacturing industries (making goods), over three-quarters of the people in London are employed in service industries such as banking, insurance, government, transport, education and food and drink.

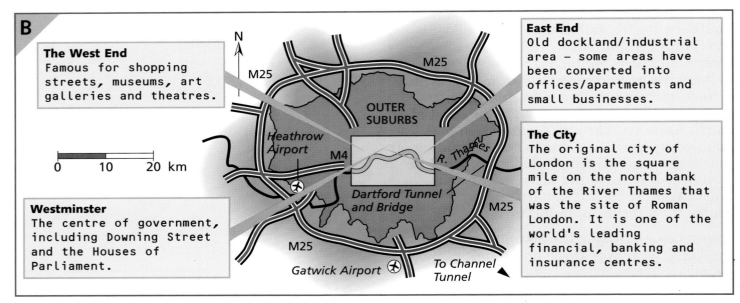

The West End
Famous for shopping streets, museums, art galleries and theatres.

Westminster
The centre of government, including Downing Street and the Houses of Parliament.

East End
Old dockland/industrial area — some areas have been converted into offices/apartments and small businesses.

The City
The original city of London is the square mile on the north bank of the River Thames that was the site of Roman London. It is one of the world's leading financial, banking and insurance centres.

Land use and transport in central London

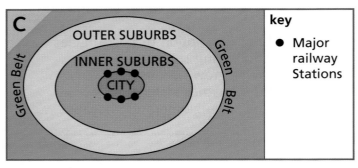

key
● Major railway Stations

Land use pattern: Most of London's six million people live in the outer suburbs

STEP 2

1 Why did London develop and grow on this site?
2 What types of industry developed in London?
3 What functions do both London and Los Angeles have?
4 How does the pattern of land use change in different parts of London?

• how processes lead to similarities and differences between places •

Problems of Los Angeles

Natural disasters have seriously damaged the environment in and around Los Angeles. There are also human problems facing people in Los Angeles.

G

There is much unemployment and poverty in the city, and as a result there were protest riots in 1965 and again in 1992. These caused huge damage to shops and buildings.

E

The motorways, or 'freeways', that criss-cross the city have created traffic congestion and smog. Smog is a mixture of smoke from all the vehicles, industries, and fog that collects in the valley. The smog is so bad that the state of California has passed laws to encourage the use of electric vehicles.

Summers are very warm and dry. In 1993 large brushfires swept through parts of the city.

D

Los Angeles is a good place to live – if you have money and a job. Thousands of people migrate there every year to look for work. In the 1990 census over one-third of the people who had moved to Los Angeles came from Mexico and Asia. Many of the migrants from Mexico entered the country illegally. In some districts over 70 per cent are black and in other areas over 70 per cent are Hispanic (mostly from Mexico). Many people in these areas are poor.

F

In 1994 a massive earthquake shook Los Angeles, killing 57 people and damaging thousands of buildings.

Houses and tenements are overcrowded. In some of these areas half the people are out of work and there are high crime rates. Problems are often connected with drug dealing and gang warfare.

Despite these problems many poor people still try to move into Los Angeles. At the same time, problems are forcing many other people to move away from the city to find work and a new home in another place.

 http://www.uk.multimap.com

STEP 3

1 Imagine you are a *rich* person living in Los Angeles. Write a letter to a friend, explaining why you are thinking of leaving the city. Include at least three reasons why you are moving.
2 Imagine you are a poorer person moving to Los Angeles. Give three reasons why you are moving.

London's problems

In the past ...

London was one of the first 'megacities'. Some people called it a 'metropolis', which means that it is a centre of trade and industry. Other people called it 'The Smoke', because the air was so polluted. The air was polluted by thousands of coal fires spewing out smoke which mixed with the fog to form smog. In 1953, thousands of people died from bronchitis when London suffered a number of bad winter smogs. Soon afterwards coal fires were banned, and smokeless coal was introduced instead.

... and now

Today traffic is a major problem both inside London and around the city on the M25 motorway. Thousands of **commuters** travel into and out of central London every day to work. Every weekday the trains and tubes are packed with people travelling during the 'rush hours', and the centre is choked with traffic. The M25 was built to try to prevent congestion, but traffic is often brought to a standstill in places by accidents and by fog.

Inside London there are problems similar to those in Los Angeles. Some inner city areas suffer from high rates of crime, unemployment and poverty. Racial tension has led to riots in the past. Community groups and government schemes have been set up to try to solve some of these problems.

Like most large cities, London needs a vast amount of raw materials like water and fuel to support all the people who live there. The city consumes over one billion tonnes of raw materials every year. It also produces huge amounts of waste – over 23 million tonnes of industrial waste, household rubbish and sewage have to be disposed of each year.

The area of land needed to support a place is described as its **footprint**. London's footprint is 20 million hectares – an area that equals almost the whole of Britain itself! (See website www.wwf–uk.org.)

A lamplighter in Blackfriars, London 1945, lighting up a smoggy street

Traffic on the M25

The results of a nail bomb in Brick Lane, a suspected racist attack

STEP 4
1 List three of London's problems.
2 Explain briefly the reasons for each problem.
3 Draw a sketch for a poster to explain London's 'footprint'.

THINKING THROUGH YOUR ENQUIRY

For this task use a whole sheet of paper or a new page in your exercise book.

First set out a table like the one below to show the similarities and differences between London and Los Angeles, and then add to your table the answers to the questions 1–8.

'A comparison between London and Los Angeles'

	London	Los Angeles
1 Location (latitude/longitude)	. . . .	. . . .
2 Site and situation	. . . .	. . . .
3 Population (millions)	. . . .	. . . .
4 Reasons for growth	. . . .	. . . .
5 Functions	. . . .	. . . .
6 Industries	. . . .	. . . .
7 Pattern of land use	. . . .	. . . .
8 Problems	. . . .	. . . .

1 Use an atlas to find the locations of London and Los Angeles and describe their locations in terms of latitude and longitude.

2 Describe or draw the site and situation for both settlements.

3 What is the total population of each city?

4 Describe the growth of population over time.

5 Each settlement has several functions. What are they?

6 List the manufacturing and service industries for each settlement.

7 Describe briefly the arrangement of different parts of each city (e.g. centre and suburbs).

8 What problems does each city face? Are they similar or different?

Homework

Find out more about *either* London *or* Los Angeles and add any extra information you can find to your table. Use the websites provided and any other resources.

Extension

- Compare London or Los Angeles with a city near you, using the same points 1–8.

- Compare the cities of London and Los Angeles, and say which city you like the most.

- Imagine you lived in one of the two cities. Write a letter to a friend living in the other city. Say which city you would prefer to live in and why.

Mention the advantages *and* disadvantages of living in each city.

 http://www.eastindiadock.co.uk/intro1.html#top

2b Settlement

• The place where I live ... ? •

Where do I live?

- Where do I live?
- What is a settlement?
- How is my settlement like other settlements, or different from them?
- Why do settlements differ?

Basotho Village, Lesotho

Morocco

Hong Kong

Paris

YOUR ENQUIRY

In this enquiry you will:
- look at the factors affecting the location and structure of settlements
- explain how and why the provision of goods and services in settlements varies
- use appropriate fieldwork techniques to collect and present your own data.

At the end of the enquiry you will make a presentation on 'The pattern and structure of our local settlement'.

What is a settlement?

A **settlement** is a place where people live and work together. Settlements vary in the number of people who live there, and in the number and types of services that go on in them. If these services are ranked or counted, settlements can be placed in an order of importance, to create a **settlement hierarchy**.

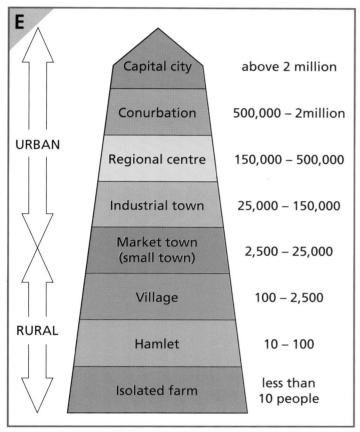

E

Settlement	Population
Capital city	above 2 million
Conurbation	500,000 – 2million
Regional centre	150,000 – 500,000
Industrial town	25,000 – 150,000
Market town (small town)	2,500 – 25,000
Village	100 – 2,500
Hamlet	10 – 100
Isolated farm	less than 10 people

URBAN

RURAL

A settlement hierarchy

Hamlets and **villages** are the smallest settlements. If there are any shops, they sell low-value items that are bought often, for example newspapers. People are not prepared to travel very far for such items. Settlements like these are found in the countryside, and are described as **rural settlements**.

Towns and cities are much larger, and have more houses and shops. They also have factories, hospitals and services that people do not use so often, so are prepared to travel further to use them. These larger built-up areas are called **urban settlements**.

F

A rural settlement

G

An urban settlement

STEP 1

1 a Do you live in a rural settlement or an urban settlement?
  b Describe the area that you live in.
2 Use a table like below to record the number and types of services in your settlement.

Food stores	. . . .
Clothes shops	. . . .
Electrical shops	. . . .

Where are settlements located?

The **location**, or **situation**, of a settlement means the place where it is found in relation to its surroundings, including other settlements and lines of communication (roads, railways). The actual land it is built on is called the **site**.

In the past, **physical factors**, including the shape of the land and the availability of food and water, were important in deciding where people lived. Then, as more and more people began to live in permanent settlements and to farm and to trade with each other, the quality and **relief** of the land, and the communication routes, became more important. Later still, as industry developed, the location of the **raw materials**, methods of transport, and **markets** for the goods produced became more important.

Today, **human factors** are the most important in locating new settlements, for example work (jobs) and good access to local services.

A

THEN ...
- Flat land.
- Good soil to farm.
- A constant water supply from a new spring or well.
- Dry land which is unlikely to be flooded.
- Shelter from the wind and rain.
- A good supply of wood for building houses and making fires.
- Defensive sites which are easy to protect from attack.

NOW ...
- A good supply of raw materials incluing coal, ore and oil.
- Good communication links, i.e. road and rail.
- Close to markets and ports.
- Where people are living.
- The cost and availability of land.

Settlement site and situation: factors affecting choice

STEP 2

You will need a 1:50,000 Ordnance Survey Landranger map of your own area.

Draw site and situation maps for your settlement. See page 39 for an example of a site map. Remember that:

- the site map should include information about height and shape (relief) of the land, and its natural features
- the situation map should include roads, railways and other settlements.

Name and give the grid reference of your settlement.

Where do people in the UK live?

In the UK, 87 per cent of the population live in towns and cities. If you fly over the country you can see that a lot of the land is built over.

In the past, most people lived and worked in the countryside. As industry developed, more and more factories were built and people moved from the countryside to the towns to find work. Today, many of the largest settlements are in places where industry used to be.

The main activity carried out with a settlement is called its function. Smaller settlements often have just one function, for example as a market town.

Most large towns and cities now have many functions – they are **multi-functional**. In the past, though, they may have grown because of just one special function, such as making something, or fishing, or tourism.

Newcastle developed because of its important docks, but it is now known for its shopping centres and its service industry.

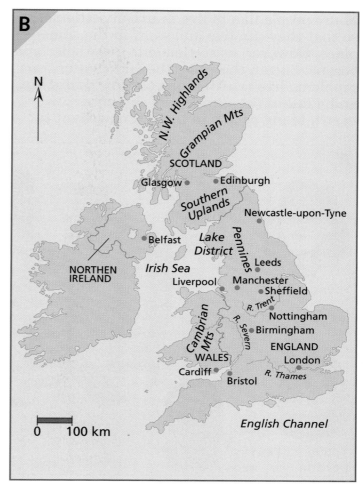

The UK's main towns and cities

STEP 3

Look at map **B**. You will also need an atlas to help you.
1 a Make a copy of map **B** and name the settlements.
  b Add your settlement to the map and also the nearest town where you go shopping.
2 a Which settlements have you visited?
  b Why did you visit these settlements?
  c Which settlements do you visit most often?
3 What is the main function of your own settlement?

Extension

Match each settlement to its main function:

A	London	1	fishing port
B	Aberdeen	2	holiday resort
C	Cambridge	3	port
D	Grimsby	4	steel manufacturing
E	Blackpool	5	university centre
F	Sheffield	6	textiles manufacturing
G	Bradford	7	oil terminal
H	Dover	8	capital city

- Do some research to find out more about one or two of these settlements.

Town v. country

Many people like to live in urban settlements so that they can live and work in the same place. However, as settlements grow older and become bigger, they often begin to suffer from problems like **traffic congestion**, **pollution**, and a fall in the **quality of the environment**. Many people in the UK now want to leave the urban areas to live in rural settlements, because they believe the environment there is better. They still have to work in towns, and so they **commute** there each day. People have different reasons for moving and opinions about the changes this has brought to the rural settlements.

• quality of rural and urban life • identifying the problems of urban growth • enquiry •

STEP 4

Make a table to show the advantages and disadvantages of living in a town or a village. Copy this table and use the comments above to complete it.

	Advantages	**Disadvantages**
Towns	Things to do like ...	
Countryside		

Homework

Create a written display to show the advantages and disadvantages of living in your settlement.

Research this display by talking to friends and family about their views. You could also take photographs or collect pictures to support your ideas.

THINKING THROUGH YOUR ENQUIRY

For this task you will need a map of your local area, for example the Ordnance Survey 1:50,000 Landranger map. Your teacher will tell you what settlement (or settlements) you are to look at, and give you information on population and services provided in the area.

The place where I live ... ?

1 What is the settlement's type and function?

- Is it a rural or an urban settlement? Explain your answer by describing its size and functions.

2 What is its location?

- Use your 'situation' map (Step 2) to describe the location of the settlement. Remember to include compass directions and a scale-line on your map. Describe the location in words, for example: 'Hilton is 8 km south-west of Derby and 4 km north of Burton upon Trent.'
- Use evidence from your 'site' map (Step 2) to explain why the site was developed, for example: 'Hilton developed because it was located on flat land, close to Sutton Brook which provided fresh water to drink and water to power the mill. It was on the main route between Derby and Uttoxeter, and inns developed here to provide a service to tired travellers.'

3 What services are provided?

- What services and/or shops are provided in your settlement (see Yellow Pages or a telephone directory)? Use the data provided by your teacher to create your own settlement hierarchy for your local area. Use diagram **E** on page 31 as a basis for your hierarchy.

4 What are the advantages and disadvantages of living here?

- Draw up a questionnaire to find out why people chose to live in your settlement, for example:
  a Why did you come to live here?
  b What are the advantages of living here?
  c What are the disadvantages of living here? Think of some other questions to ask.
- Collect your answers on a database.
- Present your findings in the form of a table or graph.

2c Settlement

• Why has Hilton village grown? •

Not In My Back Yard! (NIMBY)

- Why are people protesting about building in the countryside?

- Why can't people build houses just where they want to?

'An Englishman's home is his castle.' Traditionally, most people in the UK want to own their own home. In 1999 the government estimated that an extra 4.4 million new houses would be needed in England by 2011. But the problem of where to build them has become a matter of national debate.

Often large numbers of people feel the need to protest against new developments

YOUR ENQUIRY

In this enquiry you will:
- examine the reasons for the growth of a settlement
- consider how this growth has affected the lives of the people living there

- explore the values and attitudes of the people involved in the development.

At the end of the enquiry you will produce 'A village development plan'.

• photograph interpretation •

Why do we need more houses?

The **population structure** of the UK is changing. People are living longer, and more people are living alone, due to old age, divorce, or because they remain single. In addition, each year 90,000 people move away from towns and cities to live in the country. There are not enough houses in rural areas, so one million houses have to be built there, on **greenfield** sites. The other 3.4 million new homes will be built in areas known as **brownfield** sites.

A greenfield site

A brownfield site

B

Households in Britain

	1991	1996	2016
Total number of households (millions)	19.2	20.2	23.6
Single-person households (millions)	5.1	5.8	8.6
Average household size (number of persons)	2.47	2.39	2.17

Source: Department of the Environment, 1998

STEP 1

Look at table **B**.
1 How many more households are there likely to be in 2016 than there were in 1996?
2 Use the data to draw a line graph showing the change in single-person households.
3 Why are more people likely to live on their own in the future and what effect will this have on the types of new houses that are built?

Greenfield and brownfield sites

Greenfield sites are areas that have not yet been developed. They are found on the edges of towns and cities, or in rural areas. Brownfield sites are areas that have already been built upon, and so are found mainly in towns and cities. The government hopes that 60 per cent of all new houses will be built on brownfield sites.

Builders are being encouraged to use up this 'wasteland', where there were once factories, gas works and warehouses, before they build on precious greenfield sites. Even so, some greenfield sites will have to be used for building. Many people want to live in the country (see page 34), and there are not enough houses there. Also, most of the new houses are needed in the south-east of England, because people are moving to work in the new service and high-tech industries there. Most of the brownfield sites are in the north and the Midlands, on old industrial land.

STEP 2

Look at photographs **C** and **D**.
1 Describe each of the sites.
2 What is the difference between a greenfield site and a brownfield site?
3 What are the advantages and disadvantages of building on each site.

Homework

Design a 'dream house' for the future. Identify ways in which your design saves energy and water resources. Use pages 21 and 22 to help you.

A

Nunsfield · Fm 118 · PH · Longlane
ROMAN ROAD · 129 · 127 · The Pastures · △133 · 130 · Bowbridge House Fm · 38 · MP · 85 · Markeaton Stones
Thurvaston · Moat · N · Grange Fields Fm · Lees · PH · Langley Common · 117 · Wheathill Fm · Mackworth · Hotel · 84 · Markeaton · Crem
Butt Ho · Hall · 112 · Osleston Village · Trusleywood Ho · Foxfields Fm · Radbourne Common · 37 · Mackworth Fields · 112 · Mackworth · Coll
Oslestion · 109 · 105 · 100 ·
Broad Close · 82 · Radbourne · Silverhill Fm · 109 · Hackwood Fm · PH · dismantled railway · Sch
Churchbalk · Woodhouse Fm · 90 · Hall · 103 · 36 · Mickleover · Coll
Windle Fm · 87 · 97 · Birch Wood · 80 · Potlocks Fm · Hotel · Hospl · Hotel
Cropper · Trusley · Manor · 88 · CH · Hotel · 105
Hardley Hill · Rookhills Fm · Terrel Hays · Smerrills Fm · 90 · Wks · Sch · Littleover · 83
Lane Ends · 66 · Dalbury Hollow · Bonehill Fm · Hotel · Sch
Devil's Elbow · Trusley Brook Fm · Bearwardcote Hall · 80 · The Grange · A516(T) · 75 · 33
Baldfields Fm · Dalbury · dismantled railway · Bearwardcote Fm · Moat · PH · A525(?)
tton the Hill · 87 · Fields Fm · Highfields Fm · Hepnalls · Oakdene Fm · Burnaston · Hotel · Highfields Fm · Hall Pastures Fm
Dishfields Fm · Ashe Hall · 78 · Park Fm · New Buildings Fm · 32 · Thurston
Hilton Fields · 80 · School · Leisure Centre · Etwall · 80 · 71 · 31 · Findern · 56
71 · 68 · 57 · Hilton Lodge · Etwall Common · New Close Fm · Park Ho · 53 · 31 · Hall Brook
Burntheath · 62 · Hargate Manor · Blakeley Lodge · Car Factory · 74 · 30 · Wks · Marina · PH
Hilton · Depot · 58 · 56 · 29 · 27 · 28 · 29 · Stenson
Hall · Park Hill · LC · Wks · 42 · Power Stations · 41
Derby Airfield · Egginton Common · A38(T) · Hill Fm · Cemy · PH · A5132 · 40 · Twyf
Egginton · 53 · LC · P · X · LC · 45 · Willington · Coll · Works · Hotel · 28

0 · 1 km

38 · 37 · 36 · 35 · 34 · 33 · 32 · 31 · 30 · 29 · 28
24 · 25 · 26 · 27 · 28 · 29 · 30 · 31 · 32 · 33

Hilton and surrounding area. Reproduced from the 1999 1:50 000 Ordnance Survey map of Derby and Burton upon Trent by permission of the Controller of HMSO © Crown copyright

Hilton United – or a village of two halves?

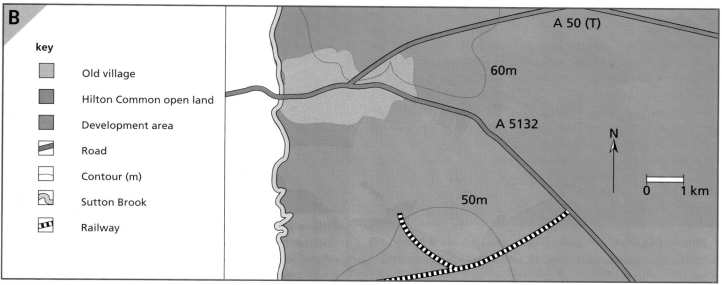

B

key

- Old village
- Hilton Common open land
- Development area
- Road
- Contour (m)
- Sutton Brook
- Railway

A 50 (T)

60m

A 5132

N

50m

0   1 km

Site of Hilton, Derbyshire

In 1992, the Japanese car company Toyota opened a large car assembly plant 6.5 km south-east of the village of Hilton, in Derbyshire. In 1994, a large housing and industrial development was started in the village. This will eventually double Hilton's size.

C	Area of land under development (hectares)	
Industrial and business use on former Ministry of Defence site		39 ha
Housing on former Ministry of Defence site		52 ha
Housing on Lucas Lane		16 ha

The site

Look at the Ordnance Survey map on page 38, and the site map **B** of Hilton. New houses are being built on two sites, both on the south side of the village centre. The larger site is on a derelict Ministry of Defence army vehicle depot (GR253298), which was a brownfield site. It lies close to the A5132, and there are railway sidings into the site coming off the main Derby–Crewe line. Internal roads, electricity, sewerage and telephone services were already provided.

STEP 3

1 Look at the Ordnance Survey map on page 38. Decide which point is probably the centre of Hilton, and give the six-figure grid reference for this point.

2 **a** Now use an atlas to find Hilton. Using this atlas and the Ordnance Survey map, draw a map to show Hilton's situation. Include Derby, Nottingham, Coventry, Milton Keynes and Northampton on your map. Add the motorway and main roads linking these places to Hilton. Include labels to indicate the distance from Hilton to each one.

  b On a copy of the site map **B**, add labels around the outside suggesting why the county planners recommended using the derelict site as a good one to build on.

Homework

1 **a** Look at table **C**. How much land is being developed within the village?

  b What proportion of it is for housing?

  c Draw a pie chart to show the proportion of land under development being used for housing, and the proportion set aside for other uses.

The old ... and the new

A

Hilton £48,000. A mature 3-bed semi-detached house requiring modernisation but benefiting from gas central heating, outbuildings and garden.

B

Hilton £92,000. Superb 4-bedroom detached house in popular new estate development with the advantages of gas central heating, double glazing, double garage and gardens. Viewing recommended.

'The locals'

The long-standing residents of Hilton tend to fall into the following categories:

- Most work in the **secondary sector** (**manufacturing**) in the engineering works in Derby, or in the service sector as nurses, teachers, shopworkers and car mechanics.
- The average age is 35–48 years old. People who have grown up in Hilton often remain after they are married. Some families have three generations living in the village, so it is a close-knit community.
- The local farmers do not live in the village, but use its services regularly. Their children like to stay in the village when they get married.

'The newcomers'

The people who are moving into the new houses have a rather different lifestyle:

- Many have well-paid, skilled jobs in the service sector. For example, there are medical, insurance and sales reps, people working in banks, offices and the computer industry, managers, technical designers, and engineers.
- Only 5 per cent of these people work at the local Toyota factory, so people either commute to work, or they work from home. Most families have two cars.
- The average age of newcomers is 28–38 years old, and many have a family. Few move into the new houses to retire.

STEP 4

1 Use the data in table **C** to draw a line graph to show the change in the number of houses in Hilton since 1994.

2 Look carefully at photographs **A** and **B**, and the site map on page 39. Describe in detail how the new housing is different from the housing in the older parts of the village. Concentrate particularly on any improvements.

3 Compare the differences between the long-standing residents and newcomers in the village.

C

Houses in Hilton, 1994–2000		
1994	**1998**	**2000**
765 houses	1286 houses	1923 houses

How is Hilton changing?

As well as the new housing, there have been other changes in the village.

• Transport

Most of the newcomers commute to work by car (see photograph **D**). Some travel as far as Coventry, Milton Keynes and even London on a daily basis. In May 1995 the village was by-passed as part of the A50 link-road improvements. The A50 was built to provide the Toyota car plant with an M1/M6 link.

It now takes less than 15 minutes to get onto the M1 from Hilton.

There is high car ownership among the newcomers

• School

The local primary school relocated to a larger site on the new development area, because the original Victorian building had become too small.

• Services

As part of the development, a £600,000 shopping parade was built within the new housing area. It includes a supermarket, a chip shop and a nursery for 90 children – there is already a waiting list. There are also plans for a family theme pub, with a beer garden and restaurant (see photograph **E**).

Planned services for the new estate

• Hilton post office

Some things do remain the same. For example, the developers of the new estate had hoped that the village post office would relocate from its central Main Street location (see photograph **F**). However, the postmistress felt it was important to remain within the heart of the existing community. Most of the people who have no transport, such as the elderly, live in the old centre.

Hilton village post office

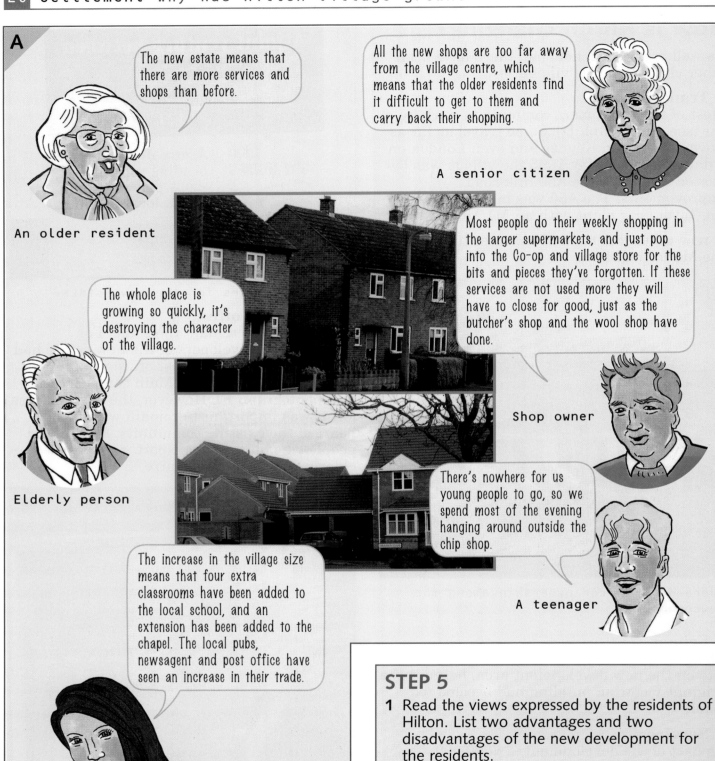

A

The new estate means that there are more services and shops than before.

An older resident

All the new shops are too far away from the village centre, which means that the older residents find it difficult to get to them and carry back their shopping.

A senior citizen

The whole place is growing so quickly, it's destroying the character of the village.

Elderly person

Most people do their weekly shopping in the larger supermarkets, and just pop into the Co-op and village store for the bits and pieces they've forgotten. If these services are not used more they will have to close for good, just as the butcher's shop and the wool shop have done.

Shop owner

There's nowhere for us young people to go, so we spend most of the evening hanging around outside the chip shop.

A teenager

The increase in the village size means that four extra classrooms have been added to the local school, and an extension has been added to the chapel. The local pubs, newsagent and post office have seen an increase in their trade.

A young mother

Villagers comment on Hilton

STEP 5

1 Read the views expressed by the residents of Hilton. List two advantages and two disadvantages of the new development for the residents.
2 Make a list of the services in the village used by the newcomers.
3 Some older residents of Hilton say that the village has 'lost its character'. What do you think they mean?

  • comparing residents' values and attitudes • drawing a plan •

THINKING THROUGH YOUR ENQUIRY

The parish council is asking for local residents' ideas on how they would like to see their community develop. Your task is to produce an A3-size village development plan, based on the village shown in the outline map **B**, and a report explaining your ideas.

'A village development plan'

Your aim:
To create a settlement that does not split the community into 'locals' and 'newcomers', but which tries to keep the existing community spirit.
- You *cannot* knock down the old village and start again, because people already live and work there.
- You *can* improve the environment by adding trees or giving the centre a 'facelift'.
- You *cannot* build on greenfield sites on the edge of the village.
- You *can* redevelop existing brownfield sites.

Before you begin to draw up your plan, think about the following key points:

1 Identify the characteristics of the local people and the newcomers who are moving into the village. (What jobs do they do? Where are the newcomers coming from? What sort of age are they likely to be?)

2 What services will the residents need? Many young people have families, so what services do they need now, and in the future?

3 What different types of housing will be needed?
- Will existing residents be able to afford the new houses? If not, what will happen to those young people who have grown up in the village and want to stay there?
- What types of housing do older people need? What can be done to accommodate them?

4 What forms of transport will be used by the different groups of people?

5 What can be done to help existing and new residents to mix?

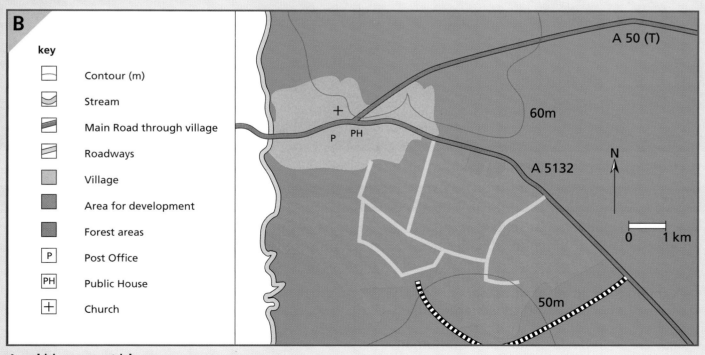

B

key

⊟	Contour (m)
⬚	Stream
▨	Main Road through village
▨	Roadways
▢	Village
▧	Area for development
▨	Forest areas
P	Post Office
PH	Public House
+	Church

A 50 (T)

60m

A 5132

N

0   1 km

50m

A village outline map

• Why was Bedford flooded? •

Flooding, people and places

• How does the weather cause flooding?   • How are people affected by flooding?

A 'RED ALERT: Bedford was last night facing the worst flooding this century'

Residential areas flooded, some residents evacuated.

Dame Alice Harpur School playing fields and buildings flooded.

Large areas of the floodplain flooded.

Suspension bridge and newly-opened butterfly bridge cut off.

Embankment walk flooded.

Bedford boathouse engulfed by water.

River Ouse floods in Bedford, April 1998

YOUR ENQUIRY

Unexpected, sudden and severe weather events can have a dramatic effect on people's lives and on the natural environment. In this enquiry you will:
• examine the causes of flooding
• explain how changes in the weather affect rivers
• describe the effects of flooding on human activities.

At the end of the enquiry you will produce a newspaper report:

'The 1998 flood in Bedford'.

This will identify the causes of the flood and explain how the weather affected Bedford and the people living there.

The flood and the people

B

FLOOD CHAOS

During the weekend fire-fighters dealt with over 350 emergency calls. One brave fireman even risked his own life to rescue two teenagers who had stolen a pleasure-boat at the height of the floods. Four people were plucked from the swollen river in Bedford and another was rescued at Priory Marina after his boat started to drift.

Reinforcements from other areas had to be drafted in to help, dealing with lightning strikes and road accidents. Seventy-five soldiers helped to hand out over 20,000 sandbags.

C Eye-witness account:

Mrs Bacon, who has lived in her home next to the river for 30 years, said: 'Everyone was taken by surprise. We put sandbags across the doorway, but when the water reached it, the water started coming through the walls and up through the floor. At first we tried to mop up the water, but had to call the fire brigade to pump it out. We decided that we would stay in the house, and went upstairs. I have never experienced a flood like this before. The last big flood was in 1947 and people said that it wouldn't happen for another 125 years. Somebody got it wrong.'

D Facts and figures: The Bedford Flood 1998

- Forty-five houses flooded, some by up to 1.2 m.
- Nine non-residential buildings flooded.
- Large areas of the floodplain flooded.
- Tesco superstore evacuated but escaped flooding by centimetres.
- Travelling funfair in Mill Meadows engulfed by water in a matter of hours. Caravans moved but rides and stalls had to be abandoned.
- Fifteen electricity sub-stations closed down and 500 homes plunged into darkness.

- Fertiliser used by farmers washed off the fields and into rivers, possibly affecting drinking-water supplies.
- Animals moved to safety.
- Crops damaged.
- Army handed out over 20,000 sandbags.
- River dumped a fine mud on the land.
- People in a state of shock as floodwater swept through their homes.
- Personal items damaged or destroyed.
- Items too big to move upstairs, like carpets, furniture and kitchen units, damaged.

STEP 1

Look at sources **A–D**, then copy and complete the following table to show how the flood affected people and the natural environment (the land and vegetation).

Human impacts (people)	Physical impacts (land and vegetation)
people evacuated	fine mud dumped on the land

Why do rivers flood?

Rivers are bodies of water that flow across the land in **channels**. As the amount of water reaching a river increases due to heavy rainfall, the level of the water rises. Very little rain falls directly into rivers. Most falls on the ground and flows either through or across the land until it joins a river (see page 53).

How does the weather affect flooding?

There are three main ways in which weather events can cause **flooding**.

1 If there is a sudden violent storm with heavy rain, the water may fall so fast that it cannot be absorbed into the ground. Instead it flows very quickly over the land and directly into rivers. This causes flash flooding. **Flash floods** are dangerous because they happen so quickly.

2 If large amounts of rain fall over a long period of time, the soil becomes **saturated**. This means that the soil can hold no more water, so the water flows over the ground into the river.

3 When temperatures rise in the spring, any snow or ice lying on the ground thaws. Again, the soil becomes saturated and there is suddenly a lot of water flowing over the land into rivers.

River Great Ouse

The Great Ouse starts 130 km west of Bedford. The land above Bedford (that is, upstream) is mainly clay. Clay is an **impermeable** rock, which means that it does not let water flow through it. During times of heavy rain, the water flows over the surface and reaches the river quickly. The land is mainly used for grazing animals or to grow crops. The river flows through a number of villages, and through the towns of Buckingham, Newport Pagnell and the centre of Bedford. Where there are settlements, the vegetation has been removed and replaced by concrete and tarmac. These surfaces are also impermeable.

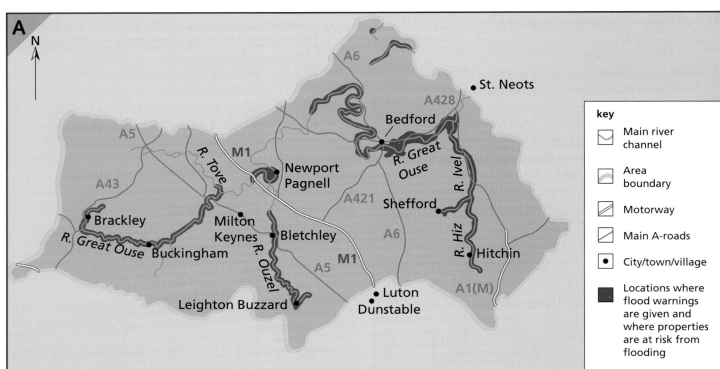

Course of the River Great Ouse: areas most at risk from flooding

 • using climate data • drawing bar charts • analysing data •

Bedford's flood, 1998

B

Rainfall for Bedford, 1998												
Month	**Jan.**	**Feb.**	**Mar.**	**Apr.**	**May**	**Jun.**	**Jul.**	**Aug.**	**Sep.**	**Oct.**	**Nov.**	**Dec.**
Rainfall (mm)	48.6	5.4	46.2	136	7.8	110.6	25.0	37.4	97.0	72.8	56.8	58.8

Source: Environmental Agency

April 1998 was the wettest month in the UK since 1818, with an overall average of 134 mm of rain. It was also the coldest April since 1989, with an average temperature of 7.7°C.

On 9 April 1998, nearly one month's rainfall fell in less than 13 hours in Bedford. Unfortunately the ground was already saturated from the above-average levels of rain that had fallen in March. The river level peaked at 26.18 m – 8 m higher than its usual level.

C

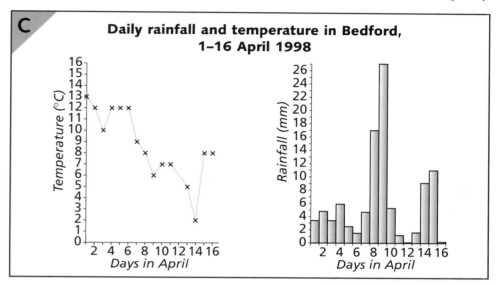

Daily rainfall and temperature in Bedford, 1–16 April 1998

D

Climate figures for Bedford, April and June 1998			
	Temperature	**Average amount of sunshine**	**Average evaporation level**
April	12.2°C	4.2 hours	1.7 mm
June	19.3°C	5.1 hours	3.3 mm

STEP 2

1 What were the average temperature and rainfall figures in April for Bedford and the UK. Describe the difference between them.

2 a Draw a bar chart to show rainfall for Bedford in 1998.
  b What was the average amount of rainfall for the year? Draw this amount as a horizontal red line on your graph.

3 a Which month had most rainfall?
  b What was the total rainfall for March and April?
  c What would be the effect of this rain on the soil?

4 Look at graph **C**.
  a On what day was the highest temperature?

b On what day was the lowest temperature?
c What was the rainfall on those days?
d Can you see any relationship between the patterns of rainfall and temperature?

Homework

Suggest why the River Ouse did not flood in June, even though there was more rainfall than there had been in April. (Hint: Think about how, during the summer when the temperature rises, the rain may have been stopped from getting into the river.)

Flow and flood

The amount of water flowing within a river is called its discharge. If the level of water rises above the top of the river bank, it spills over onto the land beyond, causing a flood. If we measure the discharge of a river over a longer period of time, it is possible to produce a graph to show the river's average flow, or **regime**.

Table **A** shows the differences in the flow of the River Ouse over a year.

A	Annual pattern of flow in the River Ouse, 1998											
Month	Jan.	Feb.	Mar.	Apr.	May	Jun.	Jul.	Aug.	Sep.	Oct.	Nov.	Dec.
Flow (m3/second)	32	9	16	57	8	13	6	5	8	17	37	35

Source: Environmental Agency

The River Ouse in normal flow

A graph that shows the flow of a river over a short period of time is called a hydrograph.

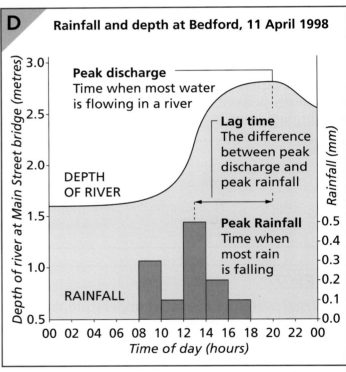

D Rainfall and depth at Bedford, 11 April 1998

Peak discharge
Time when most water is flowing in a river

Lag time
The difference between peak discharge and peak rainfall

DEPTH OF RIVER

Peak Rainfall
Time when most rain is falling

RAINFALL

Depth of river at Main Street bridge (metres)
Rainfall (mm)
Time of day (hours)

Hydrograph showing the discharge of the River Ouse

The River Ouse in flood

STEP 3

1 Use the figures in table **A** to draw a line graph showing the annual flow in the River Ouse at Bedford.
2 Draw vertical lines on your graph to show the four seasons. Label each season on your graph.

3 Using your graph, describe the pattern of the River Ouse's average flow over 1998.
4 Look back at your work in Step 2. Then, below your graph, add labels to explain how the weather affected the flow of the river.

• drawing a line graph • using river flow data • reading a hydrograph •

STEP 4

1 Look carefully at the information on page 48, then write definitions of each of the following:

- regime
- flood
- hydrograph
- peak discharge
- peak rainfall
- lag time.

2 Look at graph **D**.
  a When did the water in the River Ouse reach its peak discharge?
  b How long did it take for the river to rise from peak rainfall to peak discharge (i.e. what is the lag time)?

THINKING THROUGH YOUR ENQUIRY

You have been asked to write a newspaper article about 'The 1998 flood in Bedford'. Your editor has allowed you a double-page spread.

Here is the suggested format for your article, but you may add your own ideas:

The 1998 flood in Bedford
MAIN HEADING

Picture to show the river flooded.

- Brief description of what a flood is, and why it happened in Bedford.
- Quotations from eye-witnesses.

- Description of damage caused by the flood – effects on the natural and human environments.

Small headline

Map of the course of the River Ouse.

Small headline

- Explanation of how the weather caused the river to rise and flood.

Graph to show climate details.

You could use a DTP to help you make your pages look more professional. The presentation of your article is important, and you need to think about the whole article, not just the main headings. Make it as interesting and attractive as possible, with figures and illustrations (in colour) as well as text.

Extension

Find a newspaper report on a flood in this country or in another part of the world, e.g. on the Internet. What information and links with the weather and rainfall does the article contain (effects? causes? results? attempts to cope with the effects on people?)

3b Weather and climate
• What is weather? •

Whatever the weather ...

We often take the weather for granted, unless something dramatic happens, like a storm, a heat wave or heavy snowfall.

• When did weather last make the news?

• How does the weather affect you? How does it affect other people?

• How do weather forecasters predict the weather?

A Storms kill four

Hurricane-strength winds leave trail of death and destruction

Storm damage at Caravan Park in Northumberland

Four people were killed and a fifth was last night feared dead after hurricane-force winds of up to 170 km per hour lashed Britain and Ireland over the Christmas period.

Gale-force winds caused car crashes in Ireland. One man was swept into a rain-swollen river in Devon. Another man was dragged out to sea by a 9 m wave on the south coast. In Scotland a girl was struck by a falling chimney-stack.

All over Ireland and Scotland and parts of northern England, thousands were left in the dark as power lines were brought down. Train services were hit by wind, severe flooding and fallen trees.

Newspaper report, December 1998

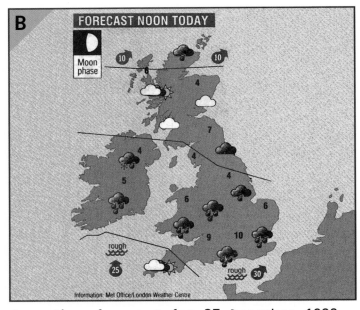

A weather forecast for 27 December 1998

YOUR ENQUIRY

In this enquiry you will:

• investigate the differences between weather and climate

• describe and explain the processes connected with the water cycle

• describe and explain patterns of weather across the UK

• describe how weather patterns and processes affect human activities.

At the end of the enquiry you will prepare 'A 24-hour weather forecast for a place in the UK'.

What do we mean by 'weather' and 'climate'?

C — What is weather?

Weather is … the *day-to-day* change in:

Aspect of weather	Description	Measurement
temperature	how hot or cold it is	measured in degrees centigrade (°C)
rainfall	how wet or dry it is	measured in millimetres (mm)
cloud cover	how much of the sky is covered	measured in eighths of the sky (oktas)
wind speed	how windy it is	measured in km per hour, or on a scale of 1 to 12
wind direction	which direction the wind is blowing from	using compass points
air pressure	how high or low the pressure is	measured in millibars (mb)

D — Weather

'Weather' describes the conditions at one place and at one time.
- The weather is different in different parts of the country.
- The weather will not be the same today as it was yesterday or will be tomorrow.
- The weather is more variable in the UK than in many other parts of the world.

E — Climate

'Climate' only changes *very slowly*, perhaps over hundreds of years.
- 'Climate' describes the average conditions in a place, which are likely to be repeated there year after year.
- In the UK it will always be cooler in winter and warmer in summer *on average*.

The UK generally has a mild, wet climate, but within the country there are differences. It is usually cooler in the north and warmer in the south. The western side of the country is generally wetter than the east.

STEP 1

1 Briefly describe your weather today. Mention if it has changed during the day. Use the list of characteristics in table **C** to help you.
2 How has the weather changed in the last few days? What is the forecast for tomorrow?
3 Watch the TV weather forecast for the next few days. Note:
   a how the weather is changing
   b what features are included in the forecasts.
4 Write two sentences to describe very carefully the differences between 'weather' and 'climate'.

Homework
- Keep a weather diary for the next two weeks. Include figures for temperature, rainfall, cloud cover, wind speed and direction, and air pressure.

  You may be able to use an automatic weather station if the school has one. Otherwise you can find the figures in newspapers, TV reports or on the Met Office website (below).

- Use the Internet or newspapers to find out what the weather is like in other parts of the world.

http://www.meto.govt.uk

Why does the weather change so often?

The weather in the UK changes very quickly and often quite dramatically. One summer day may be hot and dry, while the next is cool and wet. Snow may fall unexpectedly, even in late spring. The different areas of the atmosphere, called air masses, which surround the UK are one of the reasons for the UK's changeable weather. The British Isles are on the edge of a continent (Europe), and to the west is the Atlantic Ocean.

Where two air masses meet they form a **front**. Because of its location, many air masses and fronts pass over the UK. Fronts can move in any direction, although most come from the south and west.

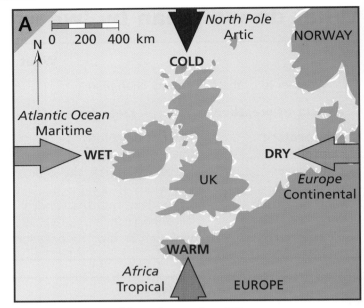

Air masses affecting the UK

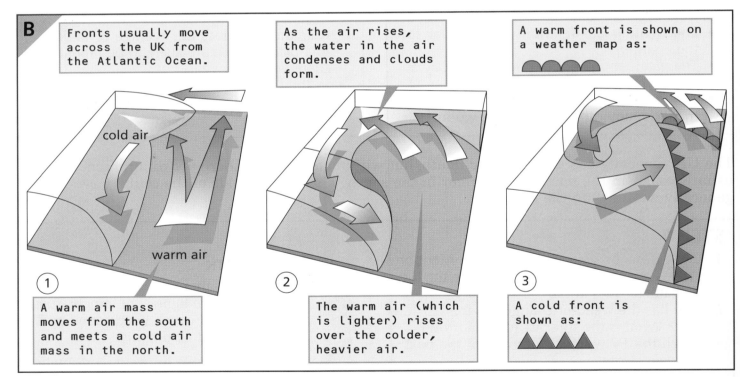

The formation of a depression

STEP 2

Look at map **A** and diagram **B**.
1 What is a front?
2 Where do fronts form?
3 What direction do they usually come from in the UK?

4 Why do clouds form along fronts?
5 Why does the UK's weather change so quickly?

      • describing weather patterns and processes •

Why does it rain?

Rain falls because water in the air (water vapour) is forced to condense. This process is described in diagram **C**.

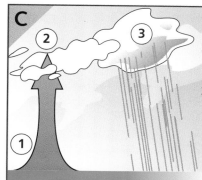

C

1 As warm air rises it cools.
2 Water in the air condenses and forms clouds.
3 Tiny droplets of water join together to form raindrops, which then fall to the ground.

Why it rains

Air can be forced to rise in three different ways. This gives the three main types of rainfall: relief, frontal and convectional (figures **D**, **E** and **F**).

D

Frontal rainfall

Where two air masses meet, the warmer air mass is forced to rise over the colder air mass. As the warm air mass rises it cools and the water contained in it condenses to form clouds.

warm   cold

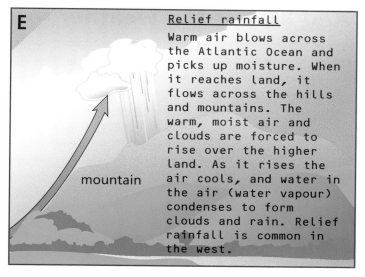

E

Relief rainfall

Warm air blows across the Atlantic Ocean and picks up moisture. When it reaches land, it flows across the hills and mountains. The warm, moist air and clouds are forced to rise over the higher land. As it rises the air cools, and water in the air (water vapour) condenses to form clouds and rain. Relief rainfall is common in the west.

mountain

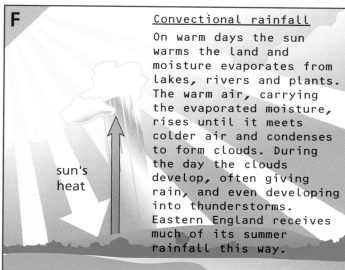

F

Convectional rainfall

On warm days the sun warms the land and moisture evaporates from lakes, rivers and plants. The warm air, carrying the evaporated moisture, rises until it meets colder air and condenses to form clouds. During the day the clouds develop, often giving rain, and even developing into thunderstorms. Eastern England receives much of its summer rainfall this way.

sun's heat

STEP 3

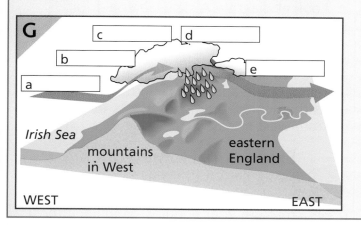

G

c   d
b
a
e

Irish Sea
mountains in West
eastern England
WEST   EAST

1 Make a copy of diagram **G**. Add the following labels in the correct boxes:
 • rising air cools
 • air rises over mountains
 • warm, moist air from the west
 • air descends and warms
 • warm air rises.
2 a Look back to the maps **A** and **B** on page 14. Describe the patterns of temperature and rainfall across the UK. Use an atlas to help you.
 b Explain the pattern on rainfall on map **B**.

http://www.meto.govt.uk/cgi-bin/ADMIN/SWXzzzzcfo

• annotating a diagram •

'And here is the weather forecast ...

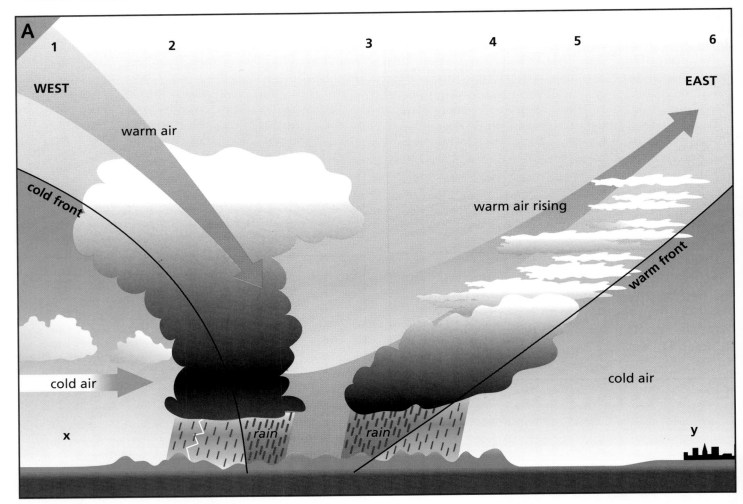

Cross-section of a depression

a	As the warm front passes, there are periods of rain.
b	As the warm front gets closer, thicker, lower-level clouds develop.
c	After the cold front has passed over, temperatures fall and there is a return to colder, clearer conditions.
d	As the warm front approaches, clouds begin to appear. The air pressure (measured on a barometer) begins to fall.
e	When the cold front arrives there is a period of heavy rain, and possibly thunder and lightning.
f	After the warm front has passed over, temperatures rise and the rain eases off.

Labels for diagram A

STEP 4

1 Look at diagram **A**. The labels **a–f** for diagram **A** are in the wrong order. Match the labels to the numbers 1–6 on the diagram.
2 You live in town **Y**. Describe the changes in temperature and rainfall you will experience as the depression moves across the town from west to east.

Extension/Homework

Listen to or watch the weather forecast for the next few days, before you think through your enquiry – and keep those weather recordings going!

... for today and tomorrow'

How do forecasters know what weather is coming our way?

By studying satellite images of air masses and fronts (photograph **B**), weather forecasters can tell us when the air masses and fronts are likely to move across the UK and change the weather. When weather forecasters look at a satellite image and see a great swirl of cloud out in the Atlantic approaching the UK, they know it is a low pressure area (a depression) bringing cloud and rain. They have to decide how quickly this low pressure area is moving, and in what direction it will travel.

Weather recordings taken around the Atlantic also give clues to the weather conditions there – the temperature, air pressure and amount of rain. From all this information, forecasters prepare maps called synoptic charts (map **C**) which show the weather conditions at a particular time.

Satellite image of a depression moving into the UK around 3.30 pm, 28 December 1998

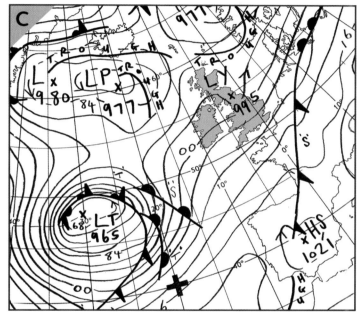

Synoptic chart of the same low pressure system at noon, over three hours earlier

STEP 5

1 Look at the synoptic chart **C**. Copy or trace the outline of the chart.
   a Mark and label the following:
   - warm front
   - cold front
   - warm sector
   - areas of cloud
   - centre of the depression.
   b Describe the shape of the cloud mass approaching the UK from the west.

   c Mark with an arrow the direction you think the depression is moving in.
2 What do you notice about the position of the low pressure system on the satellite image **B** compared with its position on chart **C**
3 Explain why a low pressure area (depression) brings cloud and rain (see pages 52–55).

 http://www.meto.gov.uk/sec3/sec3.html

 • annotating diagrams •

Why do we need weather forecasts?

Imagine you had to predict a storm – what could happen if you got it wrong?

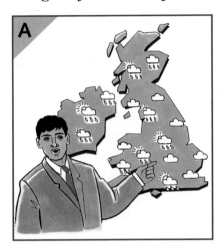

Weather presenter

The effects of mispredicted weather

The Meteorological Office sometimes gives out severe weather warnings on radio, TV and the Internet. Gale warnings are also given on the radio during the shipping forecast. These are for the main shipping areas around the coast of the UK.

C

THE LATEST WEATHER: Severe weather warning

National Meteorological Centre Bracknell
15:54 26 December 1998

EMERGENCY FLASH WARNING OF EXCEPTIONALLY SEVERE WEATHER

HERE IS AN EMERGENCY FLASH WARNING OF SEVERE GALES AFFECTING EASTERN SCOTLAND, SOUTH-WEST SCOTLAND, NORTHERN IRELAND, NORTH-EAST ENGLAND AND NORTH-WEST ENGLAND.

STORM FORCE WINDS ALREADY AFFECTING NORTHERN IRE-LAND WITH GUSTS IN EXCESS OF 160 KMPH WILL EXTEND ACROSS SOUTHERN SCOTLAND AND NORTHERNMOST COUNTIES OF NORTHERN ENGLAND RESULTING IN WIDE-SPREAD DAMAGE AND DISRUPTION.

GALE WARNING for 28 DECEMBER 1600 GMT

FASTNET
SOUTH-EASTERLY GALE FORCE 8 INCREASING SEVERE GALE FORCE 9

MAIN HEBRIDES
SOUTH-EASTERLY GALE FORCE 8 INCREASING SEVERE GALE FORCE 9

BAILEY
EASTERLY GALE FORCE 8 EXPECTED LATER

FAIR ISLE FAEROES
SOUTH-EASTERLY GALE FORCE 8 EXPECTED LATER

Weather warnings on the Internet

STEP 6

1 The cartoons (**B**) show what can happen when the weather is bad.
   a What preparations could:
      • fishermen   • travellers
      • farmers   • householders
      • the police
   make when they receive these warnings?
   b What are some possible problems and dangers if these people do *not* have an accurate forecast?
2 Look at the severe weather warnings in **C** for December 1998.
   a On an outline map of the UK, shade those areas mentioned in the warnings.
   b Use an atlas to mark on the shipping forecast areas in the gale warning, and arrows to show the direction of the storms.
   c What information does the Met Office need, in order to publish these warnings?
3 As you record the weather (especially during the winter months), note particularly any severe weather warnings from the radio or TV, or download them from the Internet.

• interpreting weather warnings • atlas skills • preparing a weather forecast •

THINKING THROUGH YOUR ENQUIRY

You may work in pairs or in groups. Your task is to prepare a weather forecast for a particular place, and describe how the weather will change there over the next 24 hours.

A 24-hour weather forecast for Y

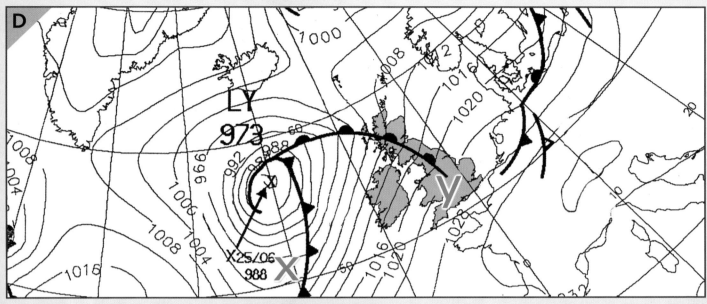

A synoptic chart for the UK, 25 November 1999

Look at map **D**. A depression is crossing the UK from the south-west. The fronts are moving across the country from west to east.

1   Describe what the weather is like now at points X and Y.

2   Prepare a weather forecast for place Y. Describe how the weather will change over the next 24 hours. Remember to describe changes in temperature, rainfall and cloud cover (see page 54).

3   Using a copy of map **D** and your own labels, present your weather forecast to the rest of the class. Use the type of language that is used by weather forecasters (look back at table **C** on page 51).

You might like to use an overhead projector, with an outline map of the UK on one sheet, and the fronts marked on another sheet. Then

you can slide the fronts across the map to show how their position will change over the next 24 hours.

4   Using the weather forecast information you have already collected, briefly explain some of the changes you are describing.

Extension

Using the Met Office website

Use a current map and satellite image to produce a weather forecast for your own area over the next 24 hours. Include in your forecast special information for particular groups of people, e.g. farmers, deep-sea fishermen, travellers, etc.

Present your weather forecast to the class as a TV or radio weather forecast. Try to use the words (vocabulary) that a weather forecaster uses.

http://www.meto.gov.uk/sec3/sec3.html
http://www.meto.govt.uk/cgi-bin/ADMIN/SWXzzzzcfo

• Can you prepare for hurricanes? •

Hurricane Georges blows its top!

- What is a hurricane?

- Where do hurricanes come from?

- How do they affect people's lives?

A 'Please, please get out while you can. For your own sake and for your loved ones, leave while you have the chance. After seeing what Andrew did, I implore you to get out.'

The Governor of Florida urges people to evacuate before Hurricane Georges arrives, 24 August 1998

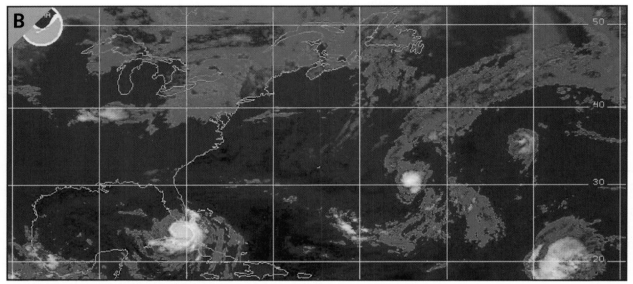

B

This is the first time that a satellite has recorded four hurricanes crossing the Atlantic at the same time. Only Hurricane Georges reached land on 25 September 1998 – it killed more than 400 people.

C

Destruction caused by Hurricane Georges in Florida

YOUR ENQUIRY

In this enquiry you will:
- describe the pattern of hurricanes across the world
- explain the processes that create a hurricane
- describe the effect of hurricanes on people's lives
- describe how people can prepare for a hurricane emergency.

At the end of the enquiry you will produce 'A hurricane disaster plan' to help reduce the risks faced by people during a hurricane.

Hurricanes

Hurricanes kill more than 20,000 people a year. Worldwide, that is more than any other form of natural disaster. A large hurricane can release more energy in one day than all the energy used in a year by the USA.

> ## STEP 1
> 1 Use a map outline of the world. On your map label all the information marked on map **D**.
> 2 Write a brief paragraph describing the world distribution of hurricanes.

Where do hurricanes occur?

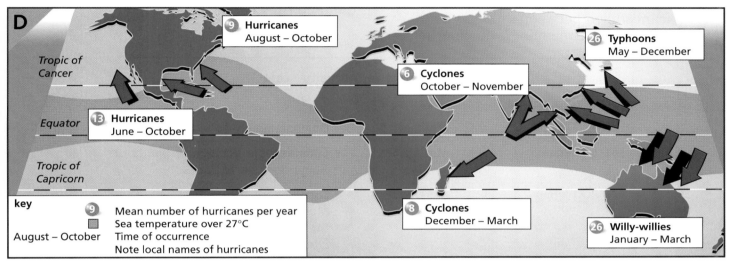

D

Tropic of Cancer

Equator

Tropic of Capricorn

9 **Hurricanes** August – October

26 **Typhoons** May – December

6 **Cyclones** October – November

13 **Hurricanes** June – October

8 **Cyclones** December – March

26 **Willy-willies** January – March

key

9 — Mean number of hurricanes per year

Sea temperature over 27°C

August – October — Time of occurrence

Note local names of hurricanes

The global distribution of hurricanes

How are hurricanes formed?

Map **D** shows that hurricanes develop in tropical areas, over the sea. Air and water are heated by the rays of the sun, which are more concentrated at or near the Equator. The hot air rises up, carrying with it large amounts of water in the form of fine droplets (**water vapour**). The warm air spirals upwards leaving an area of calm in the centre called '**the eye of the storm**'. It can be very dangerous, because as it passes over, people are fooled into thinking that the storm is over, when in fact the worst part is often still to come.

> ## STEP 2
> Look at diagram **E**.
> 1 What happens in the 'eye' of the hurricane?
> 2 Where do hurricanes develop?
> 3 Write three bullet points in the correct order to explain how a hurricane develops.

E

giant thunder clouds build up

up to 18 km high

air sinks

eye

heavy rain

heavy rain

air rises from warm ocean

air sucked in to replace rising warm air

Cross-section through a hurricane

Keeping track of events

It is very hard to predict exactly where and when a hurricane will hit, because it can develop very quickly, and change its direction and strength. The path taken by a hurricane is called its **track**.

- Hurricanes form between June and November in tropical regions in the northern hemisphere. The winds move in an anticlockwise direction.
- Hurricanes form between January and March in tropical regions in the southern hemisphere. The winds move in a clockwise direction.

Usually, when a hurricane hits land, it soon loses its energy and blows itself out.

Sizing up the problem

The size, or **intensity**, of a storm depends on its wind speed. Hurricanes are graded according to their wind speed and the level of damage they cause (table **A**).

A **The hurricane intensity scale**

Scale	Wind speed	Damage	Effects
1	120–150 kmph	Minimal	• Damage mainly to plants
2	151–170 kmph	Moderate	• Considerable damage to plants • Some damage to roofs
3	171–200 kmph	Extensive	• Large trees blown down • Mobile homes destroyed • Serious flooding of the coastline • Evacuation of low-lying coastal areas
4	201–250 kmph	Extreme	• Extensive damage to buildings • Major erosion of beaches • Major evacuation of low-lying coastal areas
5	More than 250 kmph	Catastrophic	• All trees blown down • Smaller buildings blown down • Massive evacuation of people

B **The path of Hurricane Georges, September 1998**

Date	Country	Latitude/ Longitude	Wind speed (kmph)	Category
20th	Antigua		170	2
20th	Virgin Islands		170	2
21st	Puerto Rico		180	3
22nd	Dominican Republic		190	3
23rd	Cuba		120	1
25th	Key West, Florida		165	2
27th	Biloxi, Mississippi		165	2

STEP 3

You need an outline map of the Caribbean for these activities.
1 Complete table **B**.
2 Using the information in table **B**, plot the path of the Hurricane Georges onto your outline map. Create a symbol to mark the position of the hurricane.
3 Add labels to your map to show the countries affected by the hurricane, the dates, and the wind speeds.

Extension

1 What is meant by the track of a hurricane?
2 How is the intensity of a hurricane measured?

In the Caribbean

Before ...
How did people prepare for Georges?

C Over the past 48 hours people have been getting ready for the hurricane. We have been warned to move to higher ground, and there is talk of a curfew if the hurricane hits. The supermarkets and shops have been packed with people buying things they will need if the hurricane does hit. The roads have been busy, with people leaving the area. The radio stations are broadcasting information in different languages. Most of the hurricane shelters are open, but people are having difficulty finding where they are. My dad's factory has closed.

The best thing is that school is cancelled and there is an excited atmosphere as people wait for something to happen. The government has tried to educate people about the effect of hurricanes. The 'Department of Disaster' is making sure that the country is ready – street signs have been removed, and heavy machinery is being moved into position in case it is needed once the storm has passed.

Diary entry by 12-year-old Martha, who lives in Antigua

And after ...
Hurricane Georges caused a lot of damage:
- It hit a large number of different islands. Many places were not prepared.
- A total of 467 people died, and thousands more were affected by landslides and flooding. 45 people sheltering in a school were killed when it was washed away by floodwater caused by the heavy rain.
- Bridges and roads were destroyed, making it impossible to provide immediate help.
- Hundreds of thousands of people were left homeless. Not many had insurance against such a disaster.
- Huge areas of crops, which provide food and an income, were ruined.
- Electricity and water supplies were cut off, though radio stations continued to broadcast, giving information and advice.

It was estimated that two billion US dollars would be needed to repair the damage. Many of the smaller islands did not have money set aside for emergencies. These are among the poorest countries in the world. Most of their money comes from farming and tourism, and the hurricane caused huge damage in both sectors. In the Dominican Republic 7,000 tourists arrived as soon as the airport re-opened, putting a further strain on resources. Blankets, rice, beans and fresh water were sent by other countries, and Mexico sent a plane-load of metal roofing sheets to help repair some of the damage.

'By the next morning, all wooden buildings had been destroyed and the sea had changed colour. Many buildings had been flooded, and roof tiles blown off.'

(A British tourist)

Devastation following Hurricane Georges in the Dominican Republic

STEP 4
Copy the following table, then add all the ways in which Hurricane Georges affected the Caribbean islands.

Environmental effect	landslides
Economic effects	crops destroyed
Social effects	people made homeless

In the USA

Forward planning: the key to success

The American Red Cross issues guidelines to help people prepare for a hurricane emergency.

A

Prepare for high winds

Install hurricane shutters. Make trees more wind-resistant by cutting off any damaged limbs. Stay indoors, and away from the windows.

Prepare a personal evacuation plan

Decide in advance where to go if you are told to evacuate. Keep to hand emergency telephone numbers and road maps. Listen to local radio or TV stations for evacuation advice. If advised to evacuate, leave immediately.

Assemble a disaster supplies kit

↦ First Aid kit
↦ Canned food and opener
↦ Three gallons of fresh water per person (to last at least three days)
↦ Sleeping bags
↦ Warm clothing, raincoats
↦ Battery-powered radio, torch and spare batteries
↦ Any special items needed for children, the elderly or the disabled

How to prepare for a hurricane

B

A 330-mile stretch of America's Gulf Coast is preparing for Hurricane Georges. 200,000 people have been urged or ordered to leave low-lying areas. In New Orleans high tides of 45 m are expected, and suburbs are at risk of flooding. The Red Cross is organising shelters for up to 35,000 people. Airlines have cancelled flights. Roads have been blocked with rented vans and family pick-ups loaded with possessions, as more than a million residents leave the area.

US Army troops have moved in to help police prevent looting. The Superdome football stadium, a convention centre and a massive store have been converted into hurricane shelters. Those who are staying behind have stockpiled provisions, boarded up windows and bought generators.

Evacuation before the hurricane

D ## Facts and figures

- Third most expensive storm to hit USA.
- Severe flooding along the coast.
- 2 m storm surge.
- Roads closed due to flooding/fallen trees.
- 70,000 people made homeless. Mobile homes destroyed.
- 12 counties declared 'a federal disaster'.
- Two people died because their home burnt down when they used candles for light.
- 20 mm of rain fell.
- Many ships stranded.

STEP 5

Look back over pages 61 and 62.
1 Look at figures **C**, **A** and **B**.
   a Describe the similarities in the preparations for the hurricane made by people in the Caribbean and in the USA.
   b Describe the differences in the preparations for the hurricane made by people in the Caribbean and in the USA.
2 Make a list of all the damage caused by the hurricane in the Caribbean and in the USA:

Damage in the Caribbean	Damage in the USA
467 people died	

3 Why do you think other countries sent aid to the Caribbean?
4 Try to explain why the impact of Hurricane Georges was so much greater and more disastrous in the Caribbean than in the USA.

  • comparing countries' hurricane preparations • writing a hurricane disaster plan •

THINKING THROUGH YOUR ENQUIRY

Your task is to write 'A hurricane disaster plan' in the form of a leaflet for distribution to everyone who lives in a hurricane-risk area. You need to think about:

- how the information is going to be passed on to people

- who will be involved in the operation (which particular groups)

- whether or not people will be forced (by law) to follow your advice.

Use the following outline to help you.

'A hurricane disaster plan'

1 Introduction.

- What is a hurricane?
- When is it likely to happen?
- How/why is each storm different?
- Why is it difficult to predict its track?

2 Before the storm.

- What are the problems people might face?
- How can the risks be reduced?
- What will you include in your disaster kit?
- Who will be involved in making your plan work?
- How will you inform people?

3 During the storm.

- What is your advice to people who choose to stay (are not evacuated)?
- How will you keep people informed during the storm?

4 After the storm.

- Which problems have to be dealt with first?
- Which problems can be dealt with later?

5 Summary.

- Which are the most important points of the plan? These are the points that need to go into your leaflet.

Homework

- In Japan, a lot of time is spent teaching schoolchildren what they should do in times of natural disaster.

  What methods could you use to inform children in the Caribbean or the USA about the dangers of hurricanes and what they should do when one hits?

- Imagine you live on a Caribbean island which lies in the path of the next big hurricane.

  Write a short report, to be relayed on the Internet, explaining to the rest of the world what you have done to prepare for the hurricane.

  Finish your report with a paragraph describing your own feelings as you wait.

Extension

At the time when Hurricane Georges was causing havoc in the Caribbean, there was very little world news coverage of the event. When it changed its path and headed for the USA, it suddenly became front-page news. Can you explain this?

You might like to discuss this issue with others in your class.

http://www.news.bbc.co.uk
http://www.citi-net.com/george
http://www.disasterrelief.org

http://www.disastercenter.com
http://www.caribredcross.org

4a Coasts

• Perilous paths ... or wonderful walks? •

- Where is your favourite stretch of coastline?
- What is it like?
- What makes it so special?

The Needles, off the Isle of Wight in southern England

Each section of the British coastline has its own unique character. People are attracted to coastal areas because of their wonderful views and the features produced by coastal erosion. There are many paths along the coastline of the UK, some used by people for hundreds of years. Most have spectacular views. But some are dangerous, and are falling into the sea. The coastline holds many dangers for ships too, as rocks from these eroded coasts lie just below the surface of the sea (figure **B**).

YOUR ENQUIRY

In this enquiry you will:
- describe the processes that create coastal features
- explain how these processes change coastal features
- explain how processes lead to similarities and differences between places.

At the end of the enquiry you will write 'A visitor's guide to a stretch of coastline'.

B

Hundreds of years ago, on stormy nights, people used to lure ships onto the rocks by attaching lights to cows and carts, so that it looked as if boats were safely moored in the bay. The ships came close to the shore and were wrecked. The wreckers would steal the ship's goods. On one notorious night in 1757, a total of 15 wrecks were recorded off St Catherine's Point on the Isle of Wight.

~34~

• describing and explaining a process • describing features • practising field sketching •

Coastal erosion

The blocks of chalk we call the Needles (**A**) have been worn away, or eroded, by the sea, over a long period of time. Much of the time this erosion has been gradual, but sometimes there are dramatic events. In 1764, a fourth 'Needle', which was 37m tall and known as 'Lot's wife', collapsed into the sea. People at the time heard the crash from many kilometres away.

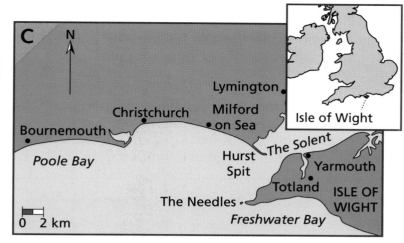

Location of the Needles off the Isle of Wight

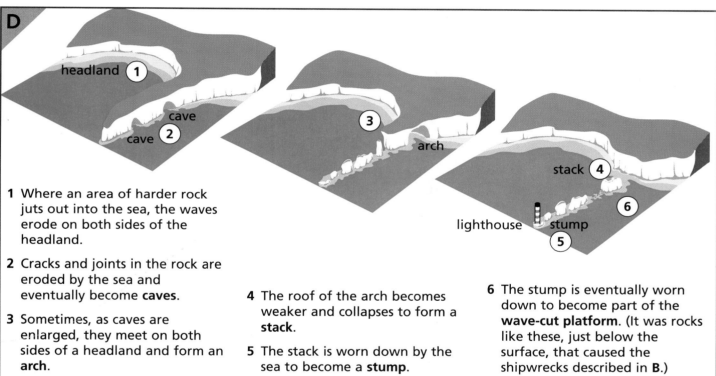

1 Where an area of harder rock juts out into the sea, the waves erode on both sides of the headland.

2 Cracks and joints in the rock are eroded by the sea and eventually become **caves**.

3 Sometimes, as caves are enlarged, they meet on both sides of a headland and form an **arch**.

4 The roof of the arch becomes weaker and collapses to form a **stack**.

5 The stack is worn down by the sea to become a **stump**.

6 The stump is eventually worn down to become part of the **wave-cut platform**. (It was rocks like these, just below the surface, that caused the shipwrecks described in **B**.)

Formation of coastal features

STEP 1

1 What are the Needles and where are they?
2 Look at photograph **A** and diagram **D**. In your own words, describe each of these features:
   • cave   • stump   • wave-cut platform.
   • arch   • stack
3 Draw a labelled sketch of diagram **D**. Add your answers to **2** as labels explaining how the Needles might have been formed.
4 Suggest what might happen to each of the stacks in photograph **A** in the future.

  http://www.netguides.co.uk

• describing and explaining a process • annotating a diagram •

Slipping and sliding into the sea

Along the south coast of the Isle of Wight there are different types of rock – chalk, sandstones and clays. Chalk is harder than sandstone and clay, and it erodes much more slowly. This difference in the speed of rock erosion is the reason for the different coastal features here, including features known locally as 'chines'. A chine is a small valley in the side of a cliff. Look for Blackgang Chine in the grid square 4876 on map **A**. Near Blackgang Chine, the coastal path follows a jumble of chalk, sandstone and clay rocks. Where different rock types meet, the cliffs are slipping and slumping down into the sea. In 1978, part of the road between Niton and Blackgang fell into the sea.

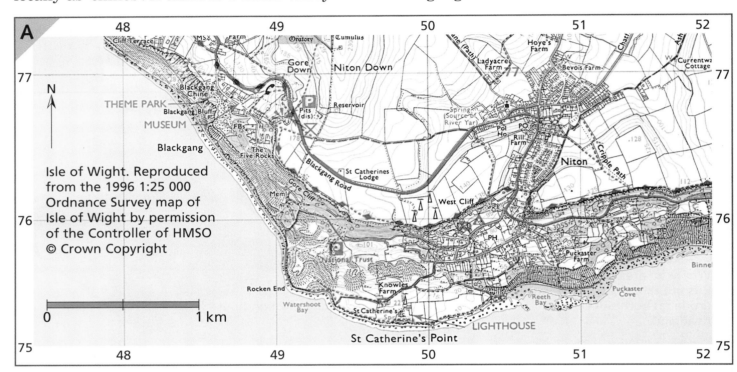

Isle of Wight. Reproduced from the 1996 1:25 000 Ordnance Survey map of Isle of Wight by permission of the Controller of HMSO © Crown Copyright

The results of a recent slip in the cliffs at Blackgang

STEP 2

Look at map **A** and photograph **B**. You may also need to refer to the Ordnance Survey map key on page 126.

1 Name the headland in grid square (GR) 4975.
2 Why does the coastal path go inland at Blackgang Chine (GR 490769)?
3 Find the coastal path in grid square 4975. What has happened to the path here?
4 Why does the coastal path need protection in some places?
5 Describe the cliffs between Cliff Terrace (GR480773) and Binnel Bay (GR518758). What features might a tourist find interesting?

The Pembrokeshire coastal path

Apart from the Needles which are made of chalk, a relatively hard rock, many of the features on the Isle of Wight are formed in soft rocks like sandstones and clays. In other parts of the UK, like Pembrokeshire in South Wales, the rocks are much harder.

C

Along the Pembrokeshire coastal path

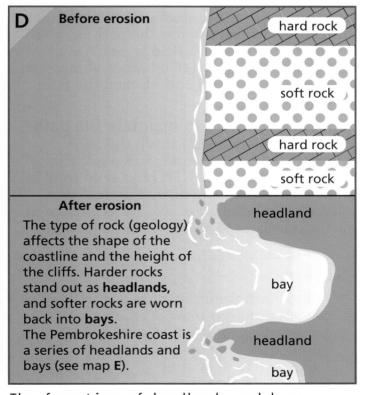

D

Before erosion

hard rock

soft rock

hard rock

soft rock

After erosion

The type of rock (geology) affects the shape of the coastline and the height of the cliffs. Harder rocks stand out as **headlands**, and softer rocks are worn back into **bays**.
The Pembrokeshire coast is a series of headlands and bays (see map **E**).

headland

bay

headland

bay

The formation of headlands and bays

  http://www.pembrokeshirecoast.org

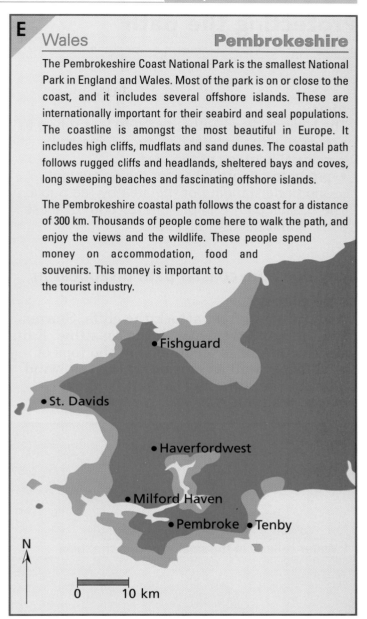

E

Wales   **Pembrokeshire**

The Pembrokeshire Coast National Park is the smallest National Park in England and Wales. Most of the park is on or close to the coast, and it includes several offshore islands. These are internationally important for their seabird and seal populations. The coastline is amongst the most beautiful in Europe. It includes high cliffs, mudflats and sand dunes. The coastal path follows rugged cliffs and headlands, sheltered bays and coves, long sweeping beaches and fascinating offshore islands.

The Pembrokeshire coastal path follows the coast for a distance of 300 km. Thousands of people come here to walk the path, and enjoy the views and the wildlife. These people spend money on accommodation, food and souvenirs. This money is important to the tourist industry.

• Fishguard

• St. Davids

• Haverfordwest

• Milford Haven

• Pembroke • Tenby

N

0   10 km

STEP 3

Look at map **E** and an atlas.
1 Name two headlands and two bays in Pembrokeshire.
2 Explain how hard rock affects the shape of the coastline in this area.
3 Why do you think the coastal path attracts so many walkers? Give at least three reasons.

Protecting the path

| A | Pembrokeshire Coast National Park |

Aims
The National Park Authority (NPA) was set up to:
- conserve the natural beauty, wildlife and cultural heritage of the area
- promote opportunities for the enjoyment and understanding of the area by the public.

The coastal path is important for both of these aims, and it needs protection.

Why does the coastal path disappear in some places?

Wind, rain and frost attack the cliffs. Storms from the south-west attack the coastline. Rain washes out gullies (channels) in the tops of the cliffs. As well as erosion by the sea, wind and rain, the rocks can be split by **frost action** (diagram **B**).

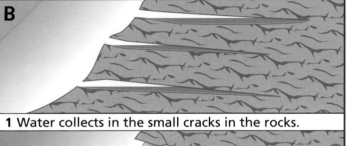

1 Water collects in the small cracks in the rocks.

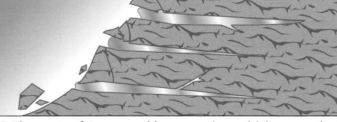

2 The water freezes and becomes ice, which expands. This exerts a force on the sides of the crack. Small pieces of rock break away. Constant freeze–thaw slowly breaks up the rock face.

3 Over a period of time, small cracks join up, and loose pieces of rock fall down the cliff.

4 Larger blocks fall down to the foot of the cliff (see photo **C**). These are then broken down by the action of the sea. Eventually they are washed away.

The process of freeze-thaw

Erosion of the coastal path near Abercastle

When erosion makes the cliff collapse, it leaves a gap in the coastal path. This makes it difficult for walkers to use the path. In one landslip, at Wiseman's Bridge near Saundersfoot, 3,000–4,000 tonnes of material slipped down the cliff and blocked the path.

What can be done to maintain the path?

Wardens and engineers check the cliffs regularly for falls. In order to keep the path open for walkers, the NPA buys land from landowners and farmers, and diverts the coastal path inland. Fences, steps and paths have to be checked and repaired regularly.

STEP 4

1 In your own words, describe and explain the process of freeze–thaw.

2 Look at diagram **D** on page 67 and photograph **C** on this page. What is happening to the clifftop?

3 What can be done to make sure the coastal path is kept open?

THINKING THROUGH YOUR ENQUIRY

During a walk along the Pembrokeshire coastal path you might see:

- small harbours that were once used for fishing, or for the export of slate and bricks
- villages with craft shops and pubs
- wildflowers and seabirds
- Bronze Age and Iron Age forts and burial chambers
- surfers, divers, sailboarders and canoeists
- wide areas of sand dunes.

Your task is to design and write a visitor's guide as a leaflet or a website for:

- *either* one of the coastal paths described in this section
- *or* an area of coastline near where you live.

You could use a desktop publishing program to produce your guide.

Refer back to the key questions on page 64 to help you make your guide as interesting as possible. Include drawings, photographs, sketch maps and cartoons in your guide. Use a website for the area to find out more information.

Use the following page plan to help you.

'A visitor's guide'

Page 1: Title

'Wonderful walks or perilous paths?'

- Include a drawing or photograph.

Page 2: Where is it?

- How can you get there (by road, by rail)? Use a road map or an atlas to describe a route from where you live.
- Draw a sketch map to show the location in the UK of the area you have chosen.

Page 3: What is the area like?

- Refer back to the work you have done for Steps 1–4. Describe the physical features, e.g. stacks, and the processes, e.g. erosion, that you might see along the walk. What wildlife might you see?

Page 4: Why do visitors come to this area?

- List at least three reasons.

How have processes formed physical features on this stretch of coast?

- Explain why the physical features are especially attractive to visitors. What other attractions might they find nearby?

 http://www.netguides.co.uk

4b Coasts

• How are coasts formed? •

Beside the seaside

- When did you last go to the beach?
- What was the beach like?
- What is your idea of the perfect beach?

Where is it?

Lulworth Cove in Dorset, on the south coast of England

YOUR ENQUIRY

In this enquiry you will:
- describe the features of the coastline
- understand how hard and soft rocks (the geology) affect erosion of the coastline
- describe and explain the physical processes that shape the Dorset coast
- discuss why this coastline needs special protection.

At the end of the enquiry you will write a report on 'Why the Dorset coast should become a World Heritage Site'.

How did it get like this?

What is it?

• describing a pattern and using key questions • photograph interpretation • field sketching

What makes this coastline so special?

One of the most famous features of the Dorset coastline is Lulworth Cove. It is well known for its geology and scenery, and is possibly the most visited site of geological interest in the UK. Many school groups and thousands of other visitors come here every year, to study the rocks and other features, to take photographs, and to draw field sketches. Like the pages of a textbook, the rocks contain the history of life (figure **B**).

Visitors also come to Dorset to walk, and to enjoy views of the sea. Along this part of the coast there are cliffs, and features such as Old Harry Rocks, which have been created by erosion of the rocks by the sea. The area is also popular for seaside holidays, and there are many camping and caravan sites along this stretch of the coast.

B

Featuring   **FOSSILS**

Dorset is famous for its fossils, especially the ones called ammonites. These fossils are the remains of creatures that lived in the sea hundreds of millions of years ago, at the time known as the Jurassic Period, when dinosaurs roamed the Earth.

C

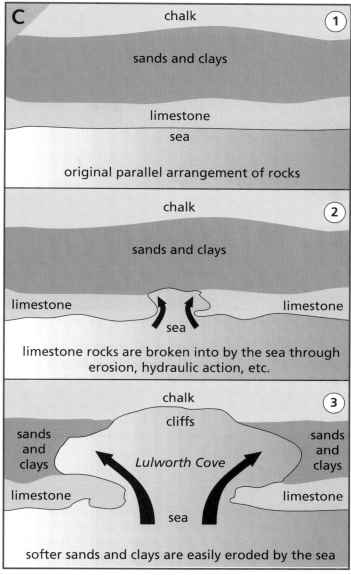

How Lulworth Cove was formed

STEP 1

1 Look at photograph **A** and diagram **C**. Describe how the pattern of hard and soft rocks affects the shape of the coast here.

2 Draw a sketch of photograph **A** and label the following features using diagram **C**:
  • the different types of rocks (limestone, chalk, sands and clays)
  • cliffs   • footpath   • car park
  • village   • Lulworth Cove.

3 Give three reasons why groups of geography students might come to Dorset to study the coastline.

Features and processes of the Dorset coastline

Old Harry Rocks off the Isle of Purbeck in Dorset

A field sketch of Old Harry Rocks

Caves, arches and stacks are often found on or near headlands. The features you see in photograph **A** are similar to the ones you looked at in the last enquiry (People and place, page 65). They are all formed by the processes of erosion acting on hard and soft rocks. One of these processes is **hydraulic action** (diagram **C**).

STEP 2

When geographers go out to study a feature they often draw a field sketch like figure **B**, to show what the feature looks like. It is usually a black-and-white pencil drawing of the main outline, with labels added. Field sketches can be used to show what you can see as well as the processes that are taking place.

Look at photograph **A**.
1 Draw your own field sketch of photograph **A**. Give your field sketch a title, and label your sketch with the following features:
   • sea   • cave   • beach
   • headland   • cliff   • arch
   • waves   • stack.   • rock
2 Now add some more labels to your sketch to show how Old Harry Rocks were formed. You may find it helpful to refer back to diagram **D** on page 65.
3 Explain briefly, in your own words, the process of hydraulic action.

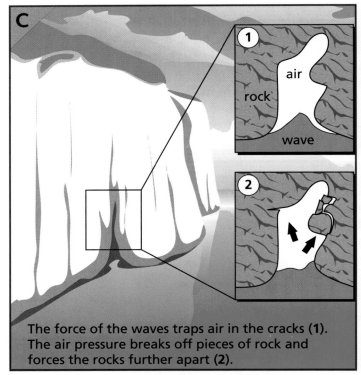

The force of the waves traps air in the cracks (1). The air pressure breaks off pieces of rock and forces the rocks further apart (2).

The process of hydraulic action

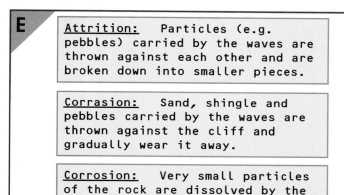

D

DORSET

Bournemouth

Durdle Door

ISLE OF WIGHT

N

Chesil Beach

• Old Harry Rocks

• Weymouth

Swanage

0   10 Kilometres

Lulworth Cove

Location of Lulworth, Old Harry Rocks and Durdle Door

E

Attrition: Particles (e.g. pebbles) carried by the waves are thrown against each other and are broken down into smaller pieces.

Corrasion: Sand, shingle and pebbles carried by the waves are thrown against the cliff and gradually wear it away.

Corrosion: Very small particles of the rock are dissolved by the sea and carried away in solution.

Durdle Door, in Dorset, and the process of erosion

The processes described in figure **E**, together with those already described, gradually erode the coast and form different features.

The pieces of rock that are worn away, or eroded, by these processes, are carried along the coast by the waves and the tides. This process is known as **transportation**.

Eventually this material (sand, shingle and pebbles) is dumped further along the coast – the process known as **deposition**. Deposition forms beaches.

http://www.csweb.bournemouth.ac.uk
    consci/coastlink/map.htm
http://www.soton-ac.uk

STEP 3

Draw a field sketch of Durdle Door. Add at least four labels to describe the processes that created this feature.

Extension

Many pupils visit the Dorset coast. Do research, and draw up a table to show places they might visit, and suggest why. You can add to this table as you work through the rest of this section. Use the websites on this page.

Place	Reasons for school field trip
Durdle Door	to look at features of coastal erosion

• annotating a field sketch • completing a table •

Chesil Beach: its formation ...

To the west of Lulworth Cove is the long stretch of shingle known as Chesil Beach (photograph **A**). Chesil Beach joins the Isle of Portland to the mainland (map **B**). Where a beach grows out from the mainland and joins onto an island it forms a feature called a **tombolo**. The beach stretches 28 km from the Isle of Portland to West Bay. Behind nearly half that length there is a tidal (saltwater) lagoon, known as the Fleet. This sheltered stretch of water is a nature reserve and provides an important habitat for animals, birds, and plants to thrive in.

It needs special protection so that threatened species can be conserved.

The sea sorts the beach material into different sizes along the length of the beach, from tiny grains of sand at Abbotsbury in the west to pebbles as large as apples at Weymouth.

The pebbles are moved along the beach by the process of **longshore drift** (diagram **C**), which is the movement of waves up the beach (swash), down the beach (backwash), and the movement of shingle along the beach.

Chesil Beach

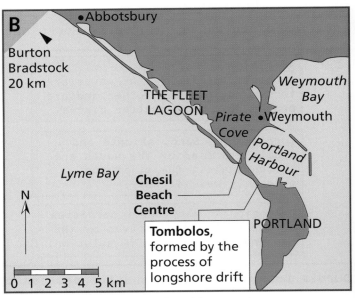

Coastal features, Chesil Beach

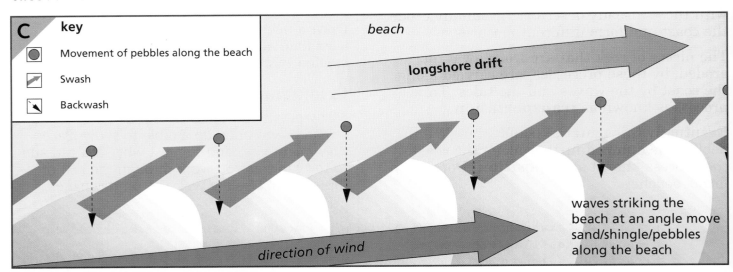

The process of longshore drift

... and flooding – a natural hazard?

D

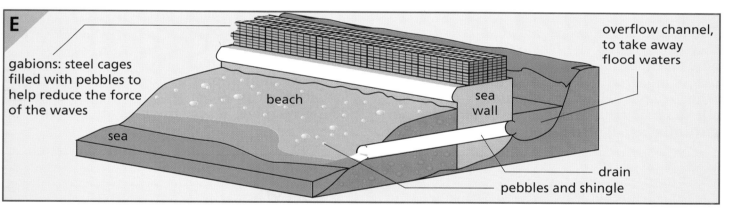

Whipped seas sever link with mainland
Worst sea flood for one hundred years!

Portland was isolated on Wednesday following a second night of storms. Hundreds of people had to be evacuated from their homes. The sea wall was breached at Chiswell and floodwaters poured through Victoria Square. Before dawn the road linking Portland was 1.2 m under water.

Flooding at Chesil Beach, December 1978: local newspaper report

Many parts of the UK's coastline are, at times, in danger of flooding. Chesil Beach is a long, continuous bank which usually forms a natural defence against the sea. Sometimes, during storms and very high tides, even this bank does not provide a secure defence. Since the storm described in newspaper article **D**, local authorities have taken measures to protect land and property from the sea in the future (diagram **E** and photograph **F**).

E

gabions: steel cages filled with pebbles to help reduce the force of the waves

beach

sea

sea wall

overflow channel, to take away flood waters

drain

pebbles and shingle

Increased flood protection

F

Flood protection measures

STEP 4

1. Look back at map **C** on page 65 and name the tombolo feature. Briefly explain the process of longshore drift.
2. Look at map **B**. With a diagram, explain why Chiswell was flooded in December 1978. Which direction do you think the storm came from? Explain your answer.
3. Imagine you live in Chiswell. Storms are forecast for the next 24 hours. Write a letter to the local newspaper describing the list of measures you have taken to prevent floods damaging your home.

 www.resortguide.co.uk

Should we protect our coasts?

A Miracle escape

Walkers had a lucky escape yesterday when hundreds of tons of rock crashed onto the beach at Burton Bradstock. The second huge cliff fall in six months buried the beach under huge sandstone boulders, filled the sky with dust and spewed a large muddy slick hundreds of yards out into the sea.

Some 1,400 tonnes of rock tumbled down to the water's edge, almost completely blocking the route to West Bay and forcing some walkers to clamber over the rocks to get back.

Local newspaper report, May 1999

Groynes on a beach

The action of the sea is continuous. Parts of the coast around the UK are being eroded almost all of the time (article **A**). In other places material is being deposited by the sea. Some people believe we should try to protect our coasts by building sea walls and placing **gabions** (see figure **E** and photograph **F** on page 75). Others believe we should encourage natural deposition by the sea by building groynes (photograph **B**). These help to slow the movement of material along the coast by longshore drift. Some people believe we should do nothing, but 'let nature take its course'.

STEP 5

1 Explain with at least two reasons why each of these people would or would not want the coast near to them protected.

   a **Mr and Mrs Walker** run a cliff-top farm. Seven years ago the farmhouse was 32 m from the cliff edge. Now the sea is just 16 m away from their front door.

   b **Brian James** is warden of a nature reserve on the Dorset coast. Many migratory birds visit his reserve because it offers the best habitat for them. The birds, animals and plants here adapt well to natural changes, but do not like to be disturbed by people.

   c **Jo Wilkes** runs a small guest-house in Chiswell, with spectacular sea-views.

2 Imagine you were one of the people in question 1. Write a brief letter to the local newspaper explaining your feelings about coastal protection.

Extension/Homework

Work in groups. Table **C** should include some of the features and processes on the coasts of the UK.

a Draw and copy of table **C**. Look back over this unit and complete the table with examples of processes and features.

b Illustrate any of the features listed in your table with drawings, photographs, or magazine cuttings. Add to this table as you find out more about coasts.

C	Coastal processes and features	
	Erosion	**Deposition**
Processes	Hydraulic action	
Features		

D   World Heritage Sites

In some parts of the world, areas have been designated World Heritage Sites. To become one, a place needs to be very special. For example, it may include:

- rocks that show changes in the evolution of animals (e.g. fossils)
- special landform features or processes (e.g. erosion)
- important habitats (e.g. the Fleet tidal lagoon).
- exceptional natural beauty (e.g. coastal scenery).

THINKING THROUGH YOUR ENQUIRY

Your task is to write a report on why the Dorset coast should be considered for a World Heritage Site. Look carefully at the factfile **D** on World Heritage Sites. Consider how each of the points can be applied to the Dorset coastline.

In your report you will need to include maps, diagrams, and sketches. (Look back at your work in Steps 1–5 of this enquiry.) Set out your report as in the outline below. If possible, use a desktop program to present your report.

'Why the Dorset coast should become a World Heritage Site'

Title

- Jurassic Coastal Park?

Introduction

- Where is it?
- What is the area like?

Section 1

- Why is this coastline special?
- Include sketches, maps, and diagrams of landforms and processes.

Section 2

- How has the coastline been formed?
- Describe some of the coastal features and processes.

Section 3

- Why is this area popular with visitors and students?
- Why do some areas need special protection? Is this from people, or from the sea, or both?

Conclusion

- Do **you** agree that the Dorset coast needs more protection and management and needs to be granted World Heritage Site status? Give three reasons, referring back to points you have made in your report.

Remember, your report needs to *convince* other people. It must be clear and persuasive.

Chesil Beach: http://www.csweb.bournemouth.ac.uk/consci/coastlink/chesilhis.htm
Lulworth Cove: http://www.soton-ac.uk

4c Coasts

• Can Hengistbury Head be protected? •

- Why do we want to protect the coast?
- Is it worth it?
- How do *you* think the area might be managed?

Saving Hengistbury Head

Hengistbury Head lies at the eastern end of Poole Bay near Bournemouth on the south coast of England (map **C**). Looking after the coast – coastal management – has been a problem in this area for many years. Over £5 million has already been spent on protecting Hengistbury Head from erosion by the sea.

A

Beach attractions at Hengistbury Head

B ## A winter walk

As you walk along the beach around the end of the headland, the string of brightly coloured beach houses stretching northwards as far as the eye can see will catch your eye. A ribbon of colour reaching out to the end of Mudeford Spit – a slender finger of land – until all you can see beyond are the white chalk stacks of the Needles.

At this time of the year, most of the houses are boarded up, with small paddle boats and oars, buckets and spades left lying outside them. The salty seaside smell really hits you as you walk towards the café for a cup of coffee.

In 1987, a series of groynes and gabions were built along this stretch of the beach to prevent the sea breaking through and flooding into Christchurch Harbour, which separates Hengistbury from the mainland.

Climbing up onto the Head itself, the views of the Needles, the Isle of Wight and Poole Bay are spectacular. The very best views are from the cliff-edge. But be careful! Severe erosion of the headland has been slowed down, but it still continues.

YOUR ENQUIRY

In this enquiry you will:
- investigate the causes of coastal erosion
- discover their effects on people's lives
- learn about ways of trying to prevent erosion.

At the end of the enquiry you will choose the best 'Coastal management plan' for Hengistbury.

Newspaper feature

Is it worth saving?

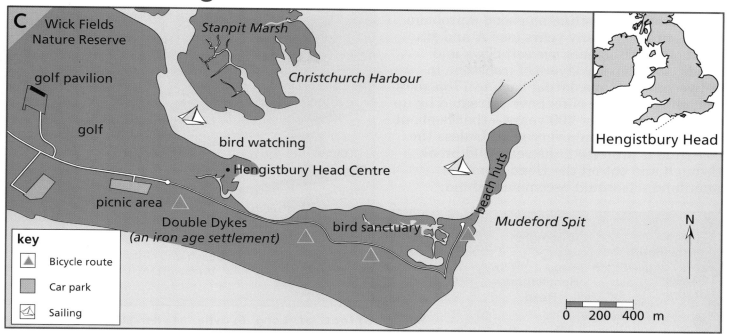

Hengistbury Head: features and attractions

D Hengistbury

- 1 million visitors a year.
- 80% come by car; most live locally.
- Owned by Borough of Bournemouth, managed by Parks and Recreation Department.
- Site of Special Scientific Interest (SSSI).
- Nature Reserve – rare plants, birds and animals.
- Important site for breeding and migrating birds.
- Ancient Monument: site of an Iron Age settlement.
- Activities: golf, cycling, sailing, riding, bird-watching, walking.

STEP 1

Look at all the information on pages 78 and 79. Imagine your family owns a beach house on Mudeford Spit. You spend a lot of time there in the summer, and your family have spent time and money repairing the house.

Write a letter to the Chief Planner of Bournemouth Council, explaining why you feel it is important that Bournemouth Council continues to protect the whole of Hengistbury Head.

http://www.the-internet-agency.com

The crumbling cliffs ...

Erosion of the coastline has been a problem in this area for many years (see **A** and **B**). Most of the cliffs here are soft clays and sands, with harder layers of ironstone in between. Old maps dating back to 1785 show that some of these cliffs have retreated by up to 100 m in the last 200 years – that is about half a metre (50 cm) every year. Unless the coastline is protected, the sea could break through and cut off the Head from the mainland – it would become an island.

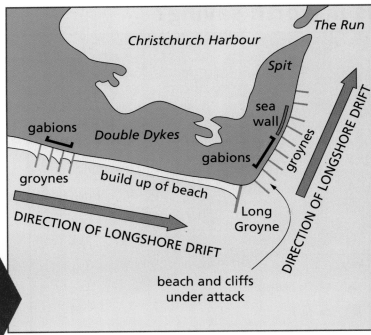

Effect of Long Groyne at Hengistbury Head

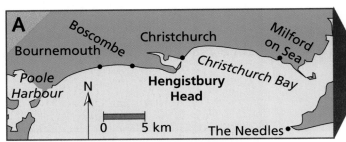

The coastline between Poole Harbour and the Needles off the Isle of Wight

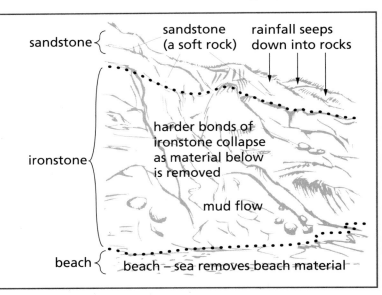

Cliffs eroding at Hengistbury Head: photograph and field sketch

STEP 2

Photograph and field sketch **B** show the features of eroding cliffs at Hengistbury and how the geology affects the cliff face. Look at these carefully, and the text above, then write a short, four-point engineers' **report** explaining how the cliffs are retreating. Start as follows:

1 The cliff is composed of ...
2 It is eroding because ...
3 The cliff face has already retreated by ...
4 Unless the cliff is protected ...

  • photograph interpretation • explaining a process • drawing a sketch map •

... and how we can protect them

The illustrations on this page (**C**) show some of the ways in which people are trying to slow the rate of erosion, and protect the coastal environment.

C

Groynes

A groyne is a barrier made of stone or wood, built out into the sea to slow the movement of beach material. As the material is moved along the beach by the process of longshore drift, some is trapped on one side of the groyne. The Long Groyne off Hengistbury Head was built in 1938. It has helped to hold back the sand, and the beach here has gradually become wider on the west (left) side. Now, though, the cliffs to the north-east of the headland are being worn away because the beach no longer receives sand and shingle that used to move around the headland. The long groyne has cut it off.

Build up of beach

Beach worn away

Where a line of groynes is built (below), the pattern of beach material is like waves.

Boscombe

Beach nourishment

On some beaches where material has been removed and not replaced, thousands of tonnes of shingle have been dredged up from the seabed offshore and pumped onto the beaches. This is known as beach nourishment.

Gabions

A gabion is a metal (wire) basket or cage filled with large stones. These break the force of the waves, and slow the movement of loose beach material. These gabions are piled up to protect the Double Dykes, an Ancient Monument.

Plants

Some plants, e.g. marram grass, are specially adapted to grow through shifting sands. This section of the beach has been fenced in against people and animals and planted with grass. The stems and roots trap blown sand and help to slow its movement. This provides a sheltered environment for plants, insects, birds and animals.

Ways we can protect our coastline: groynes, gabions and grasses

STEP 3

1 Draw a small sketch map like map **A** of Hengistbury Head to show where you think this lady has her house. Label your map to show what happens to the beach material.
2 You are the engineer for Bournemouth Council. Write in reply to this lady's complaint, explaining why the groynes were built. Use the information on page 74 to help you.

The groynes to the west of Hengistbury Head and the Long Groyne on the Head have saved the beaches to the west ... but the sand and shingle has been trapped there. Now, we are losing our beach, and cliffs at Milford on Sea further east are in danger of falling into the sea!

 • writing a report • annotating a sketch map • writing a formal letter •

A special environment

Hengistbury Head is an environmentally sensitive area containing an Ancient Monument (the Double Dykes) and a variety of important habitats. It is already an SSSI and as well as being a local nature reserve and public open space, it has been set aside as greenbelt land on the Bournemouth Council local plan. The greenbelt is an area of land that is protected from more development.

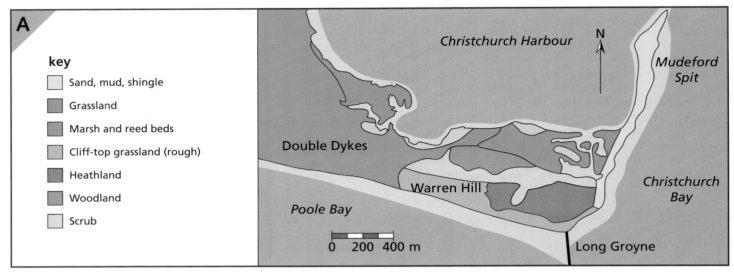

A

key

- Sand, mud, shingle
- Grassland
- Marsh and reed beds
- Cliff-top grassland (rough)
- Heathland
- Woodland
- Scrub

Christchurch Harbour

N

Mudeford Spit

Double Dykes

Warren Hill

Poole Bay

Christchurch Bay

0 200 400 m

Long Groyne

Land use at Hengistbury Head

B Hengistbury habitats

Heathland
Many animals, birds and plants, such as the smooth snake and the Dartford warbler live on the heathland.

Grassland
Rabbits graze on grass and small flowering plants. Butterflies live amongst taller, ungrazed grass which provides cover for other insects and spiders.

Scrub
Bramble provides nesting sites for birds and supports climbing plants that in turn provide nectar for bees, butterflies and hoverflies.

Woodland
The ancient woodland contains oaks and birches that attract insects and spiders, all providing food for migratory and resident birds like the great tit and the magpie.

Marsh and reed beds
The salt marshes contain an unusual mixture of salt-tolerant plants and animals. They are important feeding sites for birds like the common tern, heron, and the black-headed gull.

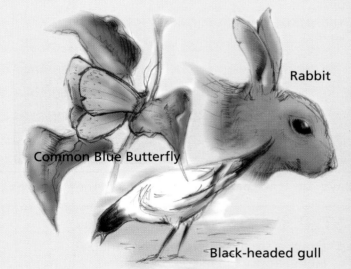

Rabbit

Common Blue Butterfly

Black-headed gull

STEP 4

1 Why is Hengistbury Head so special?
2 Why does it need to be protected?
3 How is the area protected already?

THINKING THROUGH YOUR ENQUIRY

You are a member of a committee that has been asked to decide on the best plan for managing Hengistbury Head.

Your task is to present a **report** explaining which of the following options you think is best, and why:

Option A	Let the Headland erode away naturally, and not waste money.
Option B	Continue to nourish the beach with sand and shingle, by bringing them in from offshore.
Option C	Build more gabions and groynes.
Option D	Build a sea wall all the way along the beach at the east end of Hengistbury Head.

Your report should be presented in four parts and, where possible, illustrated with maps and diagrams. Use the following steps to help you.

'Coastal management plan'

1 Introduction.

(See pages 79 and 82.)
- What is Hengistbury Head?
- Where is it?
- Why is it special?

2 Some of the main problems.

(See pages 80–82.)
- What do the residents want?
- What do visitors want?
- What about plants and wildlife?
- How are natural processes affecting the Head?

3 A solution to the problems.

- Outline the main options (**A**, **B**, **C** and **D**) available for protecting the Head.

4 Conclusion.

- Choose one of the options.
- Explain why you have chosen that option.
- Explain why you did not choose the other options.
- Sum up why a management plan is needed to protect the area.

Use the following writing frame to help you get started.

---

1 Hengistbury Head needs to be protected because:
-
-
-

2 It has several problems related to:
-
-
-

3 I think that option X is the best because ...

4 The area needs a management plan because ...

5a France

• How can Cherbourg be described? •

Welcome to France

- Where is France?
- What do you already know about France?

The Bichet family

Treauville, a small village in France

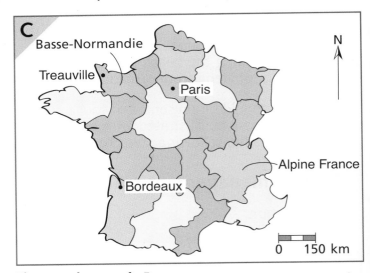

The regions of France

Meet the Bichet family, your guides to France. The Bichets live in a place called Treauville, which is a village close to the small town of Les Pieux in the Basse Normandie region of France (maps **C/D**).

Dominique Bichet was born in Paris. He is a geography teacher at a 'lycée' (secondary school) in Cherbourg. Nadia Bichet was born in Bergerac, near Bordeaux in the south-west of France. She has a job working in Flamanville Nuclear Power Station. Their children, Camille (18) and Cassandra (13), are students.

As a family, the Bichets enjoy cycling, walking, wind surfing, sand sailing and skiing (at Val d'Isère in the Alps).

YOUR ENQUIRY

In this enquiry you will:
- learn about the location, growth and functions of the town of Cherbourg
- study the character of the Cherbourg **peninsula**
- develop a knowledge of how Cherbourg is linked with other places.

At the end of the enquiry you will produce an information leaflet called 'Cherbourg and the surrounding area'.

The Cherbourg peninsula

D

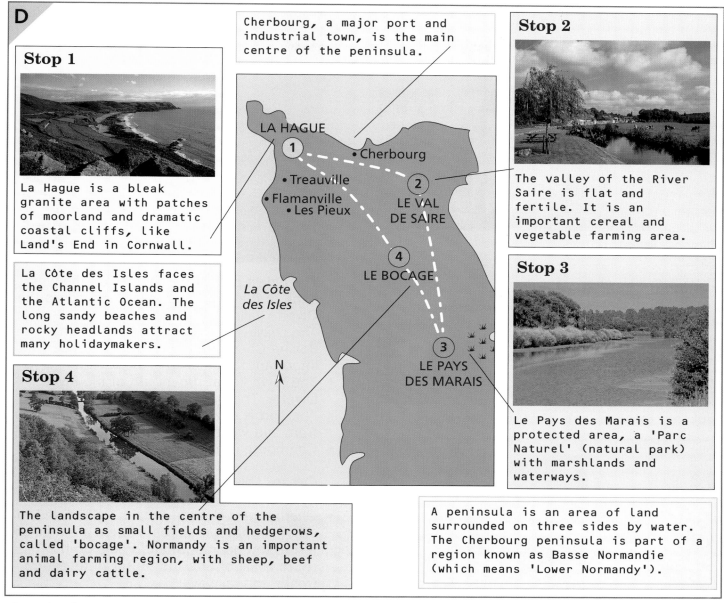

Cherbourg, a major port and industrial town, is the main centre of the peninsula.

Stop 1

La Hague is a bleak granite area with patches of moorland and dramatic coastal cliffs, like Land's End in Cornwall.

La Côte des Isles faces the Channel Islands and the Atlantic Ocean. The long sandy beaches and rocky headlands attract many holidaymakers.

Stop 4

The landscape in the centre of the peninsula as small fields and hedgerows, called 'bocage'. Normandy is an important animal farming region, with sheep, beef and dairy cattle.

Stop 2

The valley of the River Saire is flat and fertile. It is an important cereal and vegetable farming area.

Stop 3

Le Pays des Marais is a protected area, a 'Parc Naturel' (natural park) with marshlands and waterways.

A peninsula is an area of land surrounded on three sides by water. The Cherbourg peninsula is part of a region known as Basse Normandie (which means 'Lower Normandy').

The Cherbourg peninsula

STEP 1

When they first moved to Treauville, the Bichet family spent part of one school holiday cycling around the Cherbourg peninsula, getting to know their new home region. Each evening Camille and Cassandra noted in their diaries where they stopped, and what the landscape was like. The map above shows four stops on their route. Using the information on map **D**, complete a diary entry for each of these four stops. Write several sentences describing the main features of the landscape at each place.

http://www.info@normandy-tourism.org

This is Cherbourg

The town of Cherbourg is situated on the northern tip of the Cherbourg peninsula. It has developed here as a major coastal port for several reasons (see map **D** on page 85).

L'Amont Quentin

Looking towards the port of Cherbourg

Market in Place de Gaulle

Quai Alexandre III

E The growth of Cherbourg

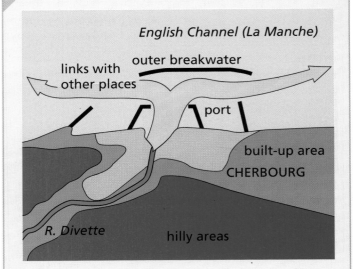

- The oldest part of the town is on the west bank of the river. It gradually spread up the Divette valley and along the coast.
- The coast is flat, and easy to build on. Behind Cherbourg there are hills, once important for defending the town.
- The town lies at the mouth of the River Divette. There is easy access to the sea.
- The port is sheltered and well protected from bad weather conditions.
- Cherbourg is next to the English Channel ('La Manche'), and close to the Atlantic Ocean. This means it has important links by sea with other places.
- Cherbourg is close to Britain, Ireland and to other countries in Europe. There are regular ferries to Portsmouth and Poole on the south coast of England. It is a **route centre** (roads and railways).

STEP 2

1 Look at the information on this page. Make a list of words that you could use to describe the geography of Cherbourg.
2 a On your list write a large letter P next to the physical features.
  b On your list write a large letter H next to the human features.
  c Use your list to help you write a clear geographical description of the town.

Spot the services

The Bichet family do most of their shopping in Cherbourg. Many **services** such as cinemas, hypermarkets, dentists, banks, restaurants and shops are used by people who live all over the Basse Normandie region. Cherbourg is, then, an important service centre.

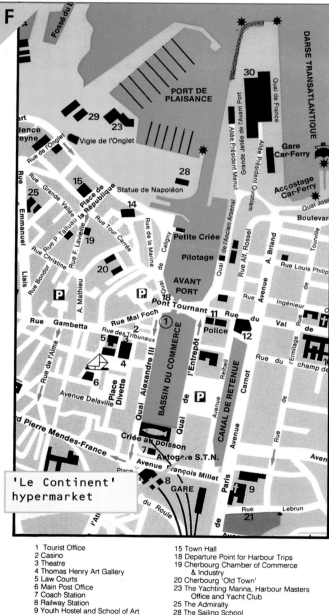

'Le Continent' hypermarket

1 Tourist Office
2 Casino
3 Theatre
4 Thomas Henry Art Gallery
5 Law Courts
6 Main Post Office
7 Coach Station
8 Railway Station
9 Youth Hostel and School of Art
11 Police Station
12 Post Office
14 Trinity Basilica
15 Town Hall
18 Departure Point for Harbour Trips
19 Cherbourg Chamber of Commerce & Industry
20 Cherbourg 'Old Town'
23 The Yachting Marina, Harbour Masters Office and Yacht Club
25 The Admiralty
28 The Sailing School
29 The Sports Centre, Skating Rink and Swimming Pool .
30 The Ferry Terminal

Cherbourg town centre

 http://www.cherbourg.com

Rue Mathieu

Quai Alexandre

STEP 3

1 What is meant by the term 'service'? What services do you have in your own area?
2 Look carefully at photographs **G** and **H**. List at least two services you can see on Quai Alexandre and in Rue Mathieu. What picture clues did you use?
3 a Using map **F**, select a pedestrian route (one you could follow on foot) from the railway station ('gare') to the town hall. What services would you pass on your walk?
  b What other services are shown on the map?
  c Why are these services found in Cherbourg?

Extension

Cherbourg has a population of about 90,000 people. What other services, not shown on map **F**, would you expect to find in a town of this size?

Sorry ... gone fishing

Trawler unloading at Cherbourg

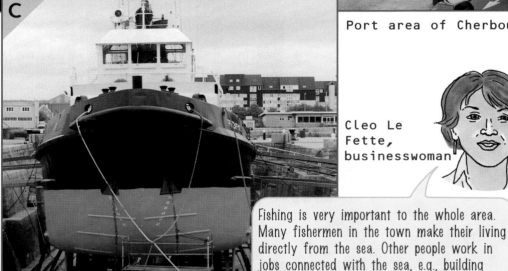
Port area of Cherbourg

Dry dock at Cherbourg

Dominique Bichet, geography teacher

One of Cherbourg's key functions is as a commercial port. Many transatlantic passenger liners dock here on their way to North America. It is a major ferry port, with links to Poole, Portsmouth and Ireland, and a cargo terminal. Raw materials such as timber and foodstuffs arrive here in containers from Africa and Asia and are processed before being sent to other places.

Cleo Le Fette, businesswoman

Fishing is very important to the whole area. Many fishermen in the town make their living directly from the sea. Other people work in jobs connected with the sea, e.g., building boats or driving lorries to deliver fish to markets in the European Union (EU), especially Belgium, Spain and Portugal. Cherbourg port has many industries: food processing, shipbuilding and repairing, marine engineering, container handling and cargo storage.

M. Peltier, local fisherman

I'm a deep-sea trawler owner. We travel across the Atlantic Ocean to fish off Newfoundland. We freeze our catch on board, and bring it back to Cherbourg to be processed, or transported by refrigerated lorry to other countries. The lobsters, crabs and shellfish caught by local fishermen are better fresh, so other lorries have special water tanks to keep them alive on their journey to such cities as Brussels and Madrid.

STEP 4

Use the information on this page to write a list showing how the port of Cherbourg is linked with other places:

a in Europe **b** in the world.

Use your library to find other links Cherbourg has. Check out atlases, encyclopedias and CDs.

Homework

Why do you think it is necessary to take boats out of the water from time to time? What jobs might have to be undertaken?

A major route centre

Cherbourg railway station

Cherbourg is an important route centre. Many roads, railways, and air and sea routes meet in Cherbourg. These, and different means of communication (telephone, cable, satellite, radio) link the town to other places in the region, in France, and in the world.

STEP 5

1 How many different types of transport can you see in photograph **D**?
2 What clues do the company logos in **E** give you about what routes and communications meet at Cherbourg? (Use a French dictionary for 'Météo'.)

THINKING THROUGH YOUR ENQUIRY

You are employed by the Normandy tourist board. You have been asked to prepare an A5 information leaflet about the Cherbourg peninsula and the town of Cherbourg for British schoolchildren.

Many groups of schoolchildren now visit this area as part of their French and geographical studies.

The leaflet must be informative, and written in a style that is easy to understand. To make it more effective and eye-catching, include maps, diagrams, and sketches.

'Cherbourg and the surrounding area'

Your leaflet must include:
- information on the location of the Cherbourg peninsula and the town of Cherbourg
- a summary of the landscapes in the peninsula (Step 1)
- information on the character of the town of Cherbourg (Step 2)
- a description of the main functions of the town (Steps 3 and 4)
- information about the links between Cherbourg and other places (Steps 4 and 5).

 http://www.meteo.fr

5b France

• How has Val d'Isère changed? •

Alpine catastrophe!

- Where are the Alps?
- What changes are taking place in the region today?
- How was the landscape affected by glaciation in the past and humans today?

'It looks like a bomb has gone off'

Source: The *Daily Telegraph*, 11 February 1999

'The whole mountainside was coming down towards us'

Source: The *Daily Telegraph*, 11 February 1999

Killer Avalanche Sweeps Away Chalets

Source: The *Daily Telegraph*, 23 February 1999

Every year the Bichet family spend their winter holidays in Val d'Isère in the French **Alps**. In 1999, though, they decided to cancel their Alpine holiday because of events there.

Destroyed by a river of snow: people dig away snow from their damaged village

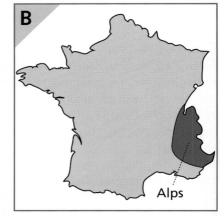

The Alps in France

YOUR ENQUIRY

In this enquiry you will:
- investigate the geography of the Val d'Isère and Tignes area of the French Alps
- recognise and describe some of the human and physical processes and patterns that have given the area its character
- investigate **avalanches**, a natural hazard that can affect the area.

At the end of the enquiry you will create an information poster display on 'Val d'Isère'.

Avalanche!

 • interpreting photographs, text and diagrams • creating diagrams •

Avalanche!

Every winter snow comes to the Alps. The date of the first heavy falls ('première neige' in French) and the amount varies from year to year. Some Alpine countries receive more snow than others. Big build ups of snow can spell disaster for countries.

D Beware avalanches!

In France, thousands of tourists are trapped after heavy snow and stormy weather cut off access to several areas. In Val d'Isère, 20,000 people were unable to leave or even ski because all 320 km of the resort's ski-runs were shut. Tignes police confirmed that 25,000 people were trapped last night as heavy snowfalls blocked the D87 road out of the resort.

Newspaper report, February 1999

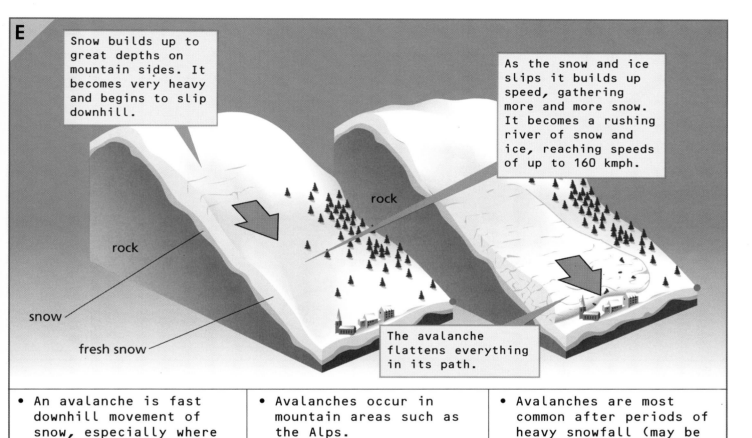

E

Snow builds up to great depths on mountain sides. It becomes very heavy and begins to slip downhill.

As the snow and ice slips it builds up speed, gathering more and more snow. It becomes a rushing river of snow and ice, reaching speeds of up to 160 kmph.

rock

rock

snow

fresh snow

The avalanche flattens everything in its path.

- An avalanche is fast downhill movement of snow, especially where slopes are steep.

- Avalanches occur in mountain areas such as the Alps.

- Avalanches are most common after periods of heavy snowfall (may be several metres).

How avalanches happen

STEP 1

1 Look at photograph **A** and the newspaper extracts on pages 90 and 91. Describe the effect avalanches have on people and places.
2 Make a diagram, with labels, to explain why avalanches happen in the French Alps.
3 Do you think the Bichet family were right to call off their 1999 winter holiday? Why?

Use http://www.météo.fr/ to catch the first snows.

http://www.abcnews.go.com/
sections include:
world/dailynews/Europe-
snow9902//.html

Off to the piste

The Bichet family travel by car from their home at Treauville in the Cherbourg peninsula to Val d'Isère. Travel through the Alps can be very difficult, especially in winter. The roads are often icy, and sometimes blocked by snow or avalanches. The high mountains also make travel difficult, and because many people visit the area, long queues can build up.

Work goes on every year, usually in the summer, to improve access to the area. It can be very expensive to widen roads, build new tunnels to more **remote** villages, and improve avalanche protection on these routes.

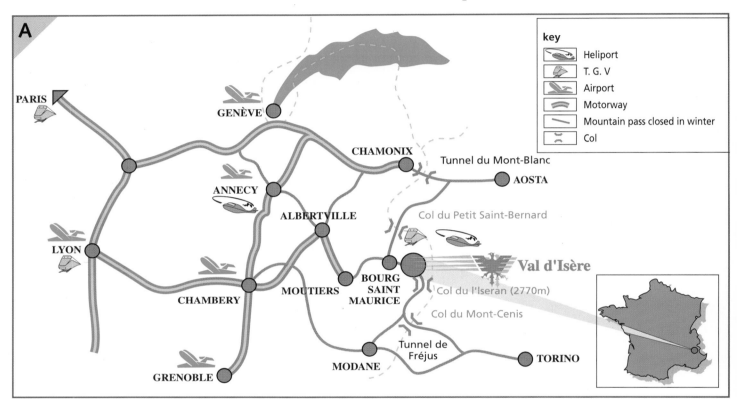

key
Heliport
T. G. V
Airport
Motorway
Mountain pass closed in winter
Col

PARIS
GENÈVE
CHAMONIX
Tunnel du Mont-Blanc
AOSTA
ANNECY
ALBERTVILLE
Col du Petit Saint-Bernard
LYON
Val d'Isère
BOURG SAINT MAURICE
Col du l'Iseran (2770m)
CHAMBERY
MOUTIERS
Col du Mont-Cenis
Tunnel de Fréjus
TORINO
MODANE
GRENOBLE

Routes to Val d'Isère

Col des Montets

STEP 2

1 **a** Describe the route you think the Bichets take when they travel from Treauville to Val d'Isère. Use map **A** and an atlas to help you.
  b How can people from other countries reach Val d'Isère? Look at map **A**.
2 Why might mountain passes such as the Col du Petit Saint-Bernard be closed during the winter months? (A **col** is a gap through the mountains, and roads are often built through them.) Look at photograph **B**.
3 How do people from Turin (Torino) in Italy reach Val d'Isère in winter?

So this is Val d'Isère!

Val d'Isère grew up on the floor of the valley of the Isère river. Like other valleys in the Alps, this is a glacial valley (photograph **C**) that was carved out (eroded) by ice during the last **Ice Age**, which ended about 25,000 years ago. The river now follows the path cut by the glaciers. Glacial erosion created this landscape, but now tourism is reshaping the area. At first people came to the area to walk, climb and see the scenery. Then, in the 1950s and 1960s, winter sports (skiing, snowboarding, tobogganing) were developed, and places like Val d'Isère and neighbouring Tignes became all-year-round resorts. Now, tourists come every year, summer and winter (mid-November to mid-April).

Sharp 'knife-edge' mountain ridges called arêtes. These were carved out by glacial erosion and frost weathering, which makes them very jagged. (P)

Avalanche barriers made of concrete or steel positioned where avalanches are most likely to happen. These stop the free slide of snow and ice, and protect routes and settlements. (H)

Road along valley floor into village. (H) Often closed due to heavy snow or avalanches. (P)

Tourism brings in a lot of money to the local economy. Tourists spend their money on ski equipment, lift passes, accommodation, food and souvenirs. (H)

High, rugged mountain peaks up to 3,500 m high, e.g. Grande Motte. These are among the highest mountains in Europe. (P)

Rocky valley sides, often cliffs. In some places waterfalls cascade to the valley floor below. (P)

Steep-sided, flat-floor valley. These huge U-shaped valleys were deepened and smoothed by glaciers during the last Ice Age. (P)

Village on valley floor. Most Alpine villages face south (that is, they are on the north side of the valley) so that they receive most sunshine. (H)

Val d'Isère

STEP 3

Look carefully at photograph **C**. Note that some labels refer to physical features (P), others to human features (H).

Camille and Cassandra's grandparents live in Paris, and have never been to the Alps. Write a letter to them from either Camille or Cassandra, describing Val d'Isère in great detail. Include a sketch to show what it is like.

(P) = physical features
(H) = human features

http://www.val-disere.net
http://www.valdisere.com
http://www.eurotrails.com

Glaciers – nature's bulldozers

During the last Ice Age, most of the Alps were covered by **glaciers**. Over many years, ice built up on the mountains and then, under the force of gravity, began to flow down the valleys. Glaciers are 'rivers of ice', and like rivers they flow downhill, erode (wear away) the landscape, transport (move) material and deposit (drop) it.

As the ice moved, it widened and deepened the Alpine valleys. Around 10,000 years ago, the valley of the Isère was filled with ice, and only the highest mountain peaks would have been visible.

A

Mer de Glace glacier in the French Alps

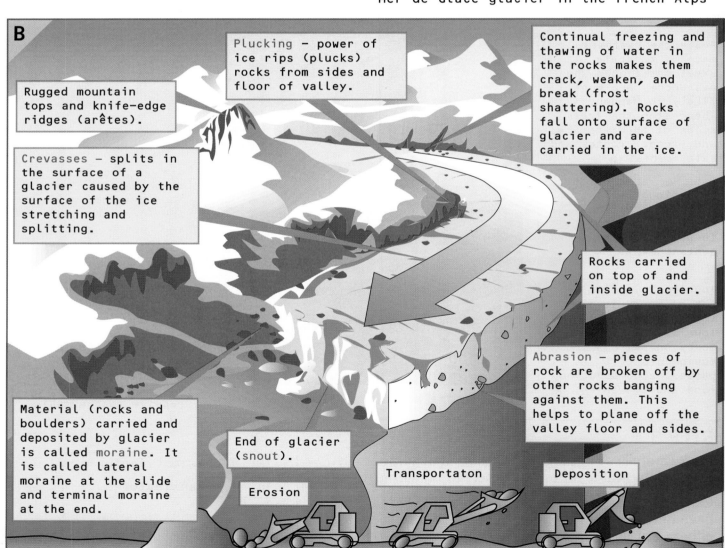

B

Plucking – power of ice rips (plucks) rocks from sides and floor of valley.

Continual freezing and thawing of water in the rocks makes them crack, weaken, and break (frost shattering). Rocks fall onto surface of glacier and are carried in the ice.

Rugged mountain tops and knife-edge ridges (arêtes).

Crevasses – splits in the surface of a glacier caused by the surface of the ice stretching and splitting.

Rocks carried on top of and inside glacier.

Abrasion – pieces of rock are broken off by other rocks banging against them. This helps to plane off the valley floor and sides.

Material (rocks and boulders) carried and deposited by glacier is called moraine. It is called lateral moraine at the slide and terminal moraine at the end.

End of glacier (snout).

Transportaton

Deposition

Erosion

Cross-section of a glacier

Taking the easy route

Like rivers, glaciers find 'the easy route' down the slope. Glaciers formed high on the mountains during the Ice Age. When they were big enough they began to move downhill, following valleys that had already been cut by rivers. The power of the glaciers eroded the valleys, and changed the shape of the valleys from a V-shape to a U-shape.

A V-shaped river valley

A glaciated Alpine valley: the steep valley sides have been smoothed by ice

The valley of the Isère, a U-shaped, glaciated valley today

STEP 4

1 Draw a sketch of photograph **A**. Add the following labels to your sketch:
   • mountain peaks and arêtes
   • snow and ice
   • rocks and debris
   • direction of glacier movement
   • crevasses.
   Add your own labels.

2 a Make a sketch of photographs **C** and **D**.
   b Use your sketches to describe the key differences between a river valley and a glacial valley.
   c Using diagram **B**, give reasons why the shape of the valley is altered.

Homework

Find out about glaciers today.
• Where are they?
• Why are they there?
• Why are the glaciers in the Alps today so much smaller than they have been in the past?

Extension

Look at photograph **E**. What is the biggest shaper of the Isère Valley today. Give reasons for your answer.

• interpreting a diagram •   • annotating a diagram • writing descriptions • explanation •   **95**

'Le plus bel espace de ski du monde'

Before winter sports really became popular in the 1970s, many Alpine valleys were remote farming communities. Places like Val d'Isère and Tignes were quiet villages – but by the end of the 20th century they had become 'the best skiing resorts in the world'.

Great change has come to these valleys, to cater for the tourists who flock to the region (diagram **A**). This change has been very rapid, taking place over just 20 or 30 years. By contrast, nature's changes (glaciation) were huge, but took thousands of years.

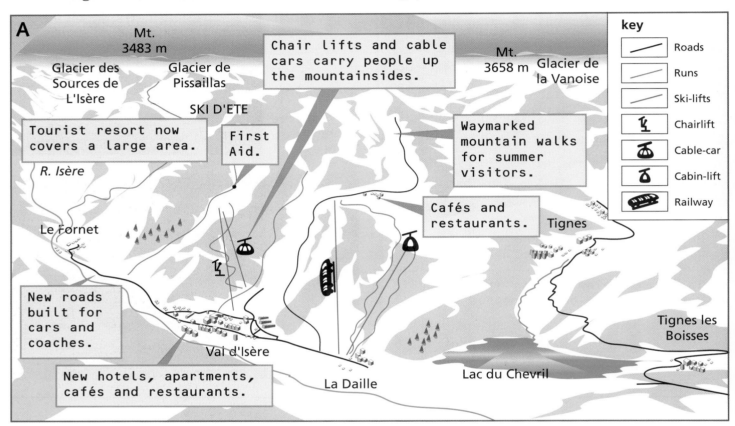

A

Mt. 3483 m

Glacier des Sources de L'Isère

Glacier de Pissaillas

SKI D'ETE

Chair lifts and cable cars carry people up the mountainsides.

Mt. 3658 m

Glacier de la Vanoise

Tourist resort now covers a large area.

First Aid.

Waymarked mountain walks for summer visitors.

R. Isère

Cafés and restaurants.

Tignes

Le Fornet

New roads built for cars and coaches.

Val d'Isère

La Daille

Lac du Chevril

Tignes les Boisses

New hotels, apartments, cafés and restaurants.

key

Roads	
Runs	
Ski-lifts	
Chairlift	
Cable-car	
Cabin-lift	
Railway	

Changes made by humans in the Isère valley

STEP 5

1 Make a sketch map of diagram **A** – leave out all the features related to tourism so that you can see more clearly the valley as it used to be..

2 a Make a list of all the features that have been added to the valley to meet the needs of tourism.

   b Describe the changes that have taken place in the valley.

3 Cassandra Bichet is doing some fieldwork as part of her school geography course. She talked to people in Val d'Isère about the changes in their lives (see **B** on page 97).

Copy and complete the table she has drawn up in her exercise book at school.

Advantages of change	Disadvantages of change
more jobs	

Extension

Suggest other advantages and disadvantages tourism brings to an area.

The process of change in the Val d'Isère and Tignes area, making it a 'winter playground' for tourists, has pleased some people, but upset others.

B

Just 30 years ago, this was a peaceful farming village. Then, we all knew everyone who lived here. Now, it's very noisy, especially at night. Even on the mountainside there are many people — before, the only sound we heard in the summer was running water and lowing cows.

A retired farmer

If it hadn't been for the development of skiing here, I would have left the village to look for a job somewhere else. Now, though, there are good jobs, and plenty to do in the evenings. My fiancé works in the ski-hire shop, which is always busy.

A young ski-instructor

Roads to and from the village are much better now. The health centre is open both to visitors and local people — we didn't have one before. We even have a cash-and-carry warehouse now.

A middle-aged hotel owner

Many of the houses and apartments are owned by outsiders now. The traditional way of life has disappeared. But we do have a regular electricity supply, and more food shops in the village.

An older woman

THINKING THROUGH YOUR ENQUIRY

'Val d'Isère'

Your task is to create a poster display telling people about the geography of the Val d'Isère and Tignes area. You should include material that answers the following questions:

1 Where is Val d'Isère? (Step 2)
2 How do glaciers shape the valley? (Step 4)
3 What are the main physical/human features of the valley today? (Step 3)
4 How has life changed for the people who live and work here? (Step 5)
5 Why did the area hit the headlines in February 1999? (Step 1)

Include map(s), sketches and diagrams to make your poster as eye-catching as possible.

Homework

Use different sources to find out about the last Ice Age.
• When did it start?
• When did it end?
• How did it affect different parts of the world?

Extension

Create a table to show how the Alpine region of France (around Val d'Isère and Tignes) is different to the Cherbourg region of Basse Normandie (pages 84 to 89). Choose your own headings. You may want to start with one labelled Location.

http://www.alpinfo.com/maps/map-fr.html

5c France

• How do places develop? •

It's Friday ... it must be market day

• What changes are taking place in your local area?

• What changes will take place in the future (new housing or roads etc.)?

People have a lot of impact on the environment. Some changes are temporary, others are permanent. The Bichet family often visit Les Pieux on market day. On market day the town centre is quite different from a normal weekday.

Les Pieux on a normal weekday

Market day at Les Pieux

YOUR ENQUIRY

In this enquiry you will:
• learn to recognise, describe and explain how people change the environment
• look at the impact of some developments in the Cherbourg and Val d'Isère regions

• decide whether or not changes to the environment are a good thing.

At the end of the enquiry you will prepare an educational TV script 'People and the environment in France'.

Off to 'Le Continent'

In Treauville, where the Bichets live, there are no shops. When they want to go shopping they travel by car to Cherbourg. There they visit Le Continent hypermarket and other large stores.

'Le Continent' hypermarket, Cherbourg

It is always busy at the hypermarket. People travel there from Cherbourg itself, from villages like Treauville, and even from the UK. It is close to the ferry port, so people can drive straight to the hypermarket, take one of the regular buses from the port, or even walk from the port.

The new hypermarket is close to the town centre, where there are picturesque old buildings and squares. It is also close to the attractive fishing harbour, and now dominates the view from the quaysides. Dominique and Nadia Bichet both feel that it looks out of place. It seems that little was done during the planning and building stages to make sure that it would blend in with the existing buildings and with the environment.

The environment of the new hypermarket

STEP 1

1 a Look at photographs **A** and **B**. What clues are there to show they were taken in the same place?

b What other changes, not seen here, might you expect to find in Les Pieux on a market day?

c Are all these changes temporary or permanent? Explain your answer.

2 Look back at the map of Cherbourg town centre on page 87. Draw a sketch to show the location of Le Continent hypermarket (it is between Quai de l'Entrepôt and Avenue Carnot, on Avenue François Millet). Add labels to show its position (e.g. close to the town centre, next to a main road, etc.).

3 Why do you think Dominique and Nadia feel that Le Continent is 'out of place'? What do *you* think?

Discuss your ideas with a partner, then add more labels to the sketch you made in question 2, commenting on its effect on the environment.

Extension

You work for Cherbourg town council. They have asked you to suggest how the hypermarket and the area around it could be improved. Use drawings to illustrate your suggestions.

A winter playground: how is it changing?

From the middle of the 20th century, the rapid growth of tourism brought many changes to the Alps. The villages of La Fornet, La Daille, Val d'Isère, Tignes and Tignes les Boisses in the Isère valley themselves changed (see pages 96 and 97), and the mountain environment was changed too.

A — Tignes today

Doctor: I remember when I could hear the sounds of birds, sheep and running water. Now all I can hear from my home is the clanking of the chairlift and the sound of endless traffic.

Farmer's wife: In the summer all you can see are very wide paths of mud and rubble on the mountainsides where the ski runs have been cut. That's where our farmland used to be.

Forester: I lost my job when the forests were cut down for the winter sports facilities. I think that's why we've been getting more avalanche damage. There are no large trees to protect the slopes and stop the flow of snow. In the summer the slopes are cluttered with chairlift supports.

Bird watcher: The number of rarer mountain birds has fallen. Their natural habitat has been disturbed and destroyed by the new tourist facilities.

STEP 2

1 Look at photograph **A**. Match each of the following labels to the photograph letters.
1 Mountainsides shaped to create ski-runs (pistes).
2 Supports for chairlifts built into the mountainside.
3 Large car park (hard surface).
4 Coach park (hard surface).
5 Flagpoles, showing European flags.
6 New hotels.
7 Avalanche fences/barriers.
8 Shops and cafés.

2 Now describe how the natural environment in and around Tignes has been changed to cater for the tourists.

The personal view

People always have different views on a changing environment. Certainly there are many different opinions about the changes taking places in villages like Val d'Isère and Tignes. The people on page 100 explain why they are not in favour of the changes. How do the views of these people above compare with those of the people on page 97?

One of the things to remember when discussing environmental issues is that it is a very personal matter – we all have different opinions. For example, did you spot the avalanche barriers on photograph **A**? On the one hand they look out of place in the natural environment. On the other hand, they have helped to protect villages and roads, and made them safer. The cost of building such barriers has been paid for by money from the tourist industry. And yet again – would avalanche barriers be necessary at all, if all the trees that used to grow here had not been cut down? There are many views on environmental issues.

Local people in Val d'Isère are especially upset about some of the new chalets and apartments, which are unsightly, and do not fit in with the village and mountain landscape. Now, much stricter planning controls are in place. People are encouraged to renovate old buildings as they become vacant, and to ensure that any new ones match the local designs and use local building materials.

Renovated farm buildings at La Fornet, Val d'Isère

New chalets and apartments at La Daille, Val d'Isère

STEP 3

1 Look at photographs **B** and **C**. Which buildings have been renovated, and which are new? Explain your answers.
2 Look carefully at photograph **A**. Try to imagine the scene *before* all the tourist facilities were built.
   a Working in pairs, write down your own thoughts about all the changes that have taken place in Tignes. Decide whether you agree or disagree with them..

b Make a classroom display of everyone's viewpoints. Then hold a class discussion called 'Are we right to keep altering the landscape? Is this really one of "le plus bel espace de ski du monde"?'.

Homework

Look at the buildings in the area where you live. Which ones do you consider 'blend' with the environment? Which do not? Try to explain your feelings. Do your friends agree with you? If not, why not?

 • debating a geographical issue • • writing descriptions • explanation • discussion/debate • **101**

Closer to home

The Bichet family like living in Treauville, a quiet village near the sea. At weekends they walk along the west coast of the Cherbourg peninsula, facing the Atlantic Ocean. Here there are cliffs and headlands, such as Cap de Flamanville, and long, deserted, sandy beaches, like the one at Sciotot. Parts of this coast are now specially protected. Here too, though, there have been changes. Since the Bichets moved to Treauville, a nuclear power station has been completed at Flamanville, and a new port and marina complex has been built at Port-Diélette.

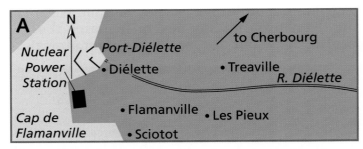

A

The Atlantic coast, Cherbourg peninsula

The new port has completely changed the coastline around the mouth of the River Diélette. Some of the money needed to build it came from EU funds. The port is expected to bring new jobs to the area, for example in operating and maintaining the port. It is also hoped that money will be made from boats visiting the port. Port-Diélette is intended to be a major international boating centre.

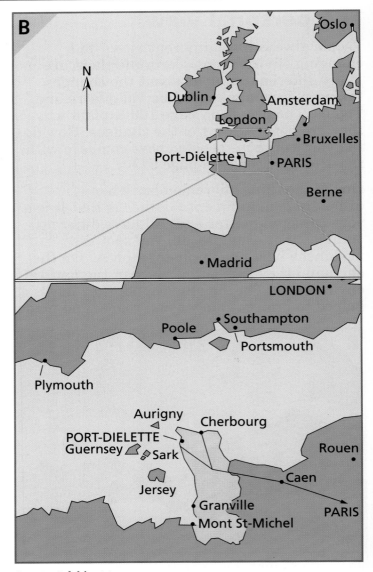

B

Port-Diélette

C Port-Diélette

- 420 floating berths (for boats moored on the water). ①
- Slipways for moving boats from the land into the water. ②
- Protective breakwaters to ensure that the port is sheltered from storms and rough seas. ③
- Large car parks to cater for weekend and holiday visitors. ④
- New roads to enable easy access to and from the port. ⑤
- Entrance lights to enable boats to navigate into the port easily.

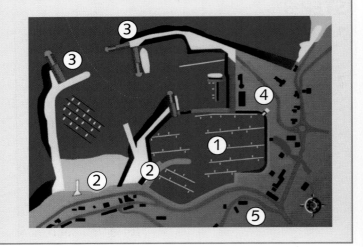

Port–Diélette

STEP 4

1 Use maps **A** and **B** to describe:
   a the *site* (local area)
   b the *situation* (wider region) of Port-Diélette
   – refer both to the local area (Cherbourg peninsula) and to the wider region (France and north-west Europe).

2 a Using photograph **D**, draw a sketch to show what the coast here would have looked like before Port-Diélette was built.

b Imagine you live in one of the old cottages beside the beach at Diélette. What would it have been like living there:
   i before the new port was built
   ii while it was being built   **iii** now?

Extension

Draw up a table of the advantages and disadvantages a new port brings.

THINKING THROUGH YOUR ENQUIRY

The TV Education Service is planning a series of short geography programmes for schools. They know that you are an expert on the effects of people on the environment. You have been asked to write a 5½-minute news item on the effects of change in the environment in Basse-Normandy and the Alps.

'People and the environment'

Your script should be structured as follows. A time-guide is given for each section. Where possible, include examples, using material from this unit (e.g. Port-Diélette or Val d'Isère).

1 Introduction.
Describe a particular example of change, e.g. the Continent hypermarket in Cherbourg.
[Time: 30 seconds]

2 Impact of change.
Describe the effects changes can have on places, e.g. people travel to the hypermarket from a wide area. This leads to more traffic.
[Time: 2 minutes]

3 Change in a particular environment.
Describe in detail the effects of change on one particular environment, e.g. the coastal environment near Port-Diélette or Val d'Isère/Tignes.
[Time: 2 minutes]

4 Conclusion.
Summarise how people have both a positive and negative impact on their environment, e.g. destroying wildlife habitats or creating safe roads to remote localities.
[Time: 1 minute]

6a Kenya
• What is Kenya like? •

Images of Africa

You may have seen pictures of Africa on TV, perhaps as part of a wildlife documentary or a programme made by Comic Relief.

• Where do our images come from?

• What is *your* image of Africa?

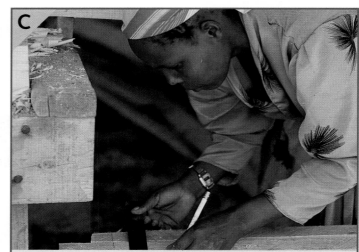

• People in the UK are often asked to give money to help projects like this in Africa. Why is this?

YOUR ENQUIRY

In this enquiry you will:
• describe the physical and human features that give Kenya its distinctive character as a country
• find out what life in Kenya is like, and how it is changing

• discover how these changes are affecting the people who live there
• learn how aid affects people in a country.

At the end of the enquiry you will write publicity material for a development agency 'How you can support a project in Kenya'.

Where is Kenya? What is it like?

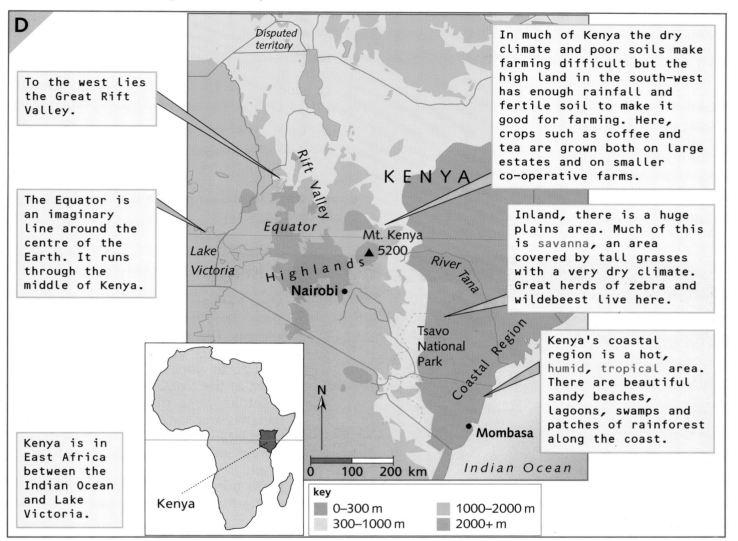

D

Disputed territory

To the west lies the Great Rift Valley.

The Equator is an imaginary line around the centre of the Earth. It runs through the middle of Kenya.

In much of Kenya the dry climate and poor soils make farming difficult but the high land in the south-west has enough rainfall and fertile soil to make it good for farming. Here, crops such as coffee and tea are grown both on large estates and on smaller co-operative farms.

Rift Valley

K E N Y A

Equator

Mt. Kenya ▲ 5200

Lake Victoria

H i g h l a n d s

River Tana

Nairobi •

Inland, there is a huge plains area. Much of this is savanna, an area covered by tall grasses with a very dry climate. Great herds of zebra and wildebeest live here.

Tsavo National Park

Coastal Region

Kenya's coastal region is a hot, humid, tropical area. There are beautiful sandy beaches, lagoons, swamps and patches of rainforest along the coast.

N

• Mombasa

Kenya is in East Africa between the Indian Ocean and Lake Victoria.

Kenya

0   100   200 km

Indian Ocean

key
0–300 m   1000–2000 m
300–1000 m   2000+ m

STEP 1

1 Use an atlas to name the five countries that surround Kenya.
2 How does Kenya's position on the Equator affect its climate (see page 119)?
3 Look at the map key showing **relief** and **elevation** (map **D**). Name the highest point in Kenya. How high is it?
4 Copy and complete the following sentences using some of the words in brackets:

a Most of the high land is in the ... (north, south, east, west).
b Most of the low land is in the ... (north, south, east, west).
5 Describe the general **pattern** of relief and elevation in Kenya.

Extension/Homework
Do research to find out more about Kenya's climate and the Great Rift Valley.

http://www.actionaid.org

Is Kenya a rich or a poor country?

Kenya is an example of a less economically developed country – an LEDC. The UK is a more economically developed country – an MEDC.

Britain ruled Kenya from 1895 until Kenya became an independent nation in 1963. A country that is ruled over by another country is called a **colony**. During the colonial period, Britain had a big influence on the economic (industry and trade) and cultural (language and education) life of the people of Kenya.

Almost all of Kenya's people are Black Africans, but there are more than 30 different ethnic groups in the country. The largest group are the Kikuyu.

Sometimes there is conflict between the different groups. In the 1980s, for example, many people were unemployed and therefore had little money, so there was public unrest.

Today, tourism is an important part of Kenya's economy. Many people work in jobs connected with tourism. Any public unrest within the country can be a big problem, because tourists do not want to visit a place that they believe could be dangerous.

A

A Kenyan lifestyle

Most Kenyan people live in rural areas. They farm the land and keep animals. The women often run small farms, called 'shambas', while the men go to work in nearby towns. Most of the crops – cabbage, potatoes, yams, maize, cassava, bananas and sugar cane – are grown for the family to eat. This is called **subsistence farming**. Any extra food is sold in the local market. These farms bring in very little money, and wages in rural areas are low.

Some **facts and figures** for Kenya and the UK show some differences between the two countries (table **B**).

B — Comparing development for Kenya and the UK

Measures of development	Kenya	The UK
Average wealth (GNP per head, US$)	270	17,970
People per doctor	10,000	300
Life expectancy (years)	Men 59	Men 73
	Women 63	Women 79
People living below the poverty line	44%	18%
Adult literacy	75%	99%
Infant mortality per 1,000 live births	64	8
Daily calorie intake	2,250 calories	3,250 calories
Access to safe drinking water	31% of people	99% of people

How is Kenya changing?

Table **B** shows that many people in Kenya do not have the things that people in the UK take for granted, for example a regular supply of food, a healthy diet, clean water, and enough hospitals, doctors and schools. In rural areas many people do not get enough to eat. Each year, many people move from the rural areas to Kenya's urban areas, hoping to raise their standard of living. The movement of people is called **migration**. People are attracted to urban areas for various reasons (figure **C**). This process is called **urbanisation**.

Urban areas are now growing rapidly, and more and more people are living in towns and cities. Nairobi, the capital of Kenya, is the largest city. It has over one million people. Many people are trapped in a **circle of poverty** (diagram **D**). In rural areas they struggle to grow enough food for themselves. In the cities they do not have access to any supply of money for housing or for running a business. Instead they have to borrow money from banks or moneylenders who charge high rates of interest.

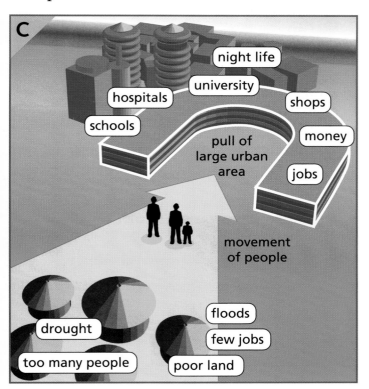

The push/pull magnet of urbanisation

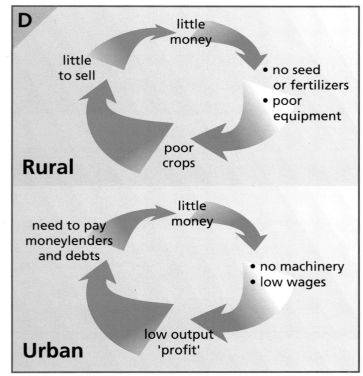

Circles of poverty

STEP 2

1 List four measures of development. Explain what you think each one means.
2 How does each of these four measures affect the life of people in Kenya?
3 Compare the lives of people in the UK and Kenya in terms of these four measures of development.

4 Imagine you live in a rural area in Kenya. You have decided to move away to work in a city. Write a letter explaining to your grandparents why you are moving away. Give at least two reasons for your decision.

 http://www.info.usaid.gov/HORN/kenya/kenya.html

Problems of living in a city

The city attracts many people, and in the wealthy central area of Nairobi there are tall office blocks, wide roads, and modern government buildings. In this area you find the parliament buildings, the Kenyatta Conference Centre, the university, and other important public buildings. But there are problems of poverty (see photograph **B**).

Kenyatta Conference Centre

Shanty housing, Nairobi

Catherine Njeri lives in Korogocho, a poor area, with her daughter Anita. Not long ago Catherine had a problem shared by many single parents in Korogocho: should she stay at home to look after her daughter, or go out and find work in order to support her? To do that she would have to leave Anita on her own or pay for child care. In Korogocho, the average wage for someone like Catherine is 90p a day. Childcare costs about the same amount of money. There are no social services, health centres or clinics in Korogocho, no roads or sewerage systems. It has the highest incidence of malaria in Kenya.

In 1993, a British development agency, Oxfam, set up an organisation to train local people as community organisers. These organisers called meetings, and the people decided that 12 women would take care of the community's children, at a rate of just 4p a day.

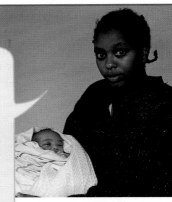

Life is hard because most people have to look for any job they can find. Many even dig pieces of land on the roadside to grow some food. Since this project started, some women have been able to go out and find work. I teach the older children to prepare them for school.

Grace Muthoni, who cares for Korogocho's children

Before the day-care centre started, I took Anita to her grandmother, who lives a long way away. Now I have more time to look for work. The day-care centre is very helpful to us, especially on health.

Catherine Njeri

ActionAid, another British development agency, has set up savings and credit groups in Korogocho. The interest rates they charge for borrowing money are cheaper than banks and moneylenders.

STEP 3

1 List the problems for people in Korogocho.
2 Why do you think it is important for people living there to find a job?
3 How have development agencies helped break the circle of poverty in urban areas (diagram **D** on page 107)?

THINKING THROUGH YOUR ENQUIRY

Imagine you are working for a development agency like Oxfam, ActionAid or Comic Relief. You have been asked to produce publicity material to encourage people in the UK to support a project in Kenya.

Using ideas from this enquiry, and also material from other sources, make up a website or a leaflet to inform people about the need to support aid projects in Kenya. You could contact some development agencies, or visit their websites.

Use the following outline to help you. You may work individually, in pairs, or in small groups.

'How you can support a project in Kenya'

Page 1

- State two of the problems facing a country like Kenya (pages 106 and 107). These might be linked to food, water or jobs.
- Explain briefly some of the reasons for these problems.
- What pictures can you include to give an idea of what the country is like? Will they give a positive or a negative impression?
- What captions or notes will you write to go with the pictures?

Page 2

- Make up a FactFile on Kenya. Include basic information on the scenery, history, the people, and the way of life.
- Include a map to show the main features of the country.

Page 3

- Describe two ways in which local people can begin to solve the problems. You will probably need to do some research for this.
- Explain how development agencies help local people to help themselves. Give examples of some projects that are happening now (again, you will need to do some research to find out about these).

Page 4

- Suggest how people in the UK can help people in Kenya. The best way is to provide the development agencies with money – try to find out some interesting figures, e.g. '£5 will pay for 100 new trees to be planted.'
  Emphasise that projects are most effective when they are organised by the local people themselves – but they need money to get started.
- Include some ideas for fund-raising (e.g. jumble sales, quiz nights, sponsored activities).

Extension/Discussion

- What is the future for young people in Kenya, like Anita Njeri (see page 108)?
- How will it be different from your future?
- What similar problems will you have? How will some problems be different?
- People today often talk about 'the global village' or 'oneworld'? What do you think this means?

http://www.actionaid.org
http://www.comicrelief.org.uk
http://www.oxfam.org.uk/atwork/where/africa/kenya.htm

6b Kenya
• How is Kenya's population changing? •

Population pressure

- Where do people in Kenya live?

- Why is Kenya's population rising so rapidly?

- What are the pressures of population growth?

A

> Many of my relatives have moved from rural areas to towns like Nairobi.

The rapid rise in population during the 1960s and 1970s in many LEDCs has been described as a **population explosion**. In the past, people in Kenya liked to have several children, to help on the family farm and, later, to support the parents in old age. But there are still large numbers of young people who are now having children of their own. The speed at which the population is increasing is now slowing down, partly because people want to have smaller families and are encouraged to use birth control. But…

Having more people means that more food has to be grown in order to feed them. This needs more land, and the land must be made to produce the amount of food that is needed. The problem for Kenya is: *can more food be produced in Kenya without damaging the environment for people in the future?*

B

Kenya's population growth, 1960–2020

1960	1970	1980	1990	2000	2020
8 million	11 million	16 million	22 million	28 million	?

YOUR ENQUIRY

In this enquiry you will:
- investigate population distribution patterns and the process of change
- describe and explain the causes and effects of population change in a country
- explain how these changes affect the lives of people
- describe and explain how population and resources are connected.

At the end of the enquiry you will write a short geographical essay called 'Describe and explain the patterns of population in Kenya'

  • interpreting graphs and statistics • drawing a graph • describing trends (patterns) •

Population means people

A **population pyramid** (diagram **C**) shows us the population structure of a country. If you compare the population pyramids for Kenya and the UK, you can see clear differences in the population structure of each country.

To construct a population pyramid you must divide up the population into males and females, and then find out how many males and how many females there are in each five-year age group. These figures are plotted as a series of horizontal bars on a graph.

The population structure of Kenya is similar to that of many other LEDCs. Its pyramid has a broad base, indicating that children and young people make up a large percentage of the population, and there are relatively few older people.

C

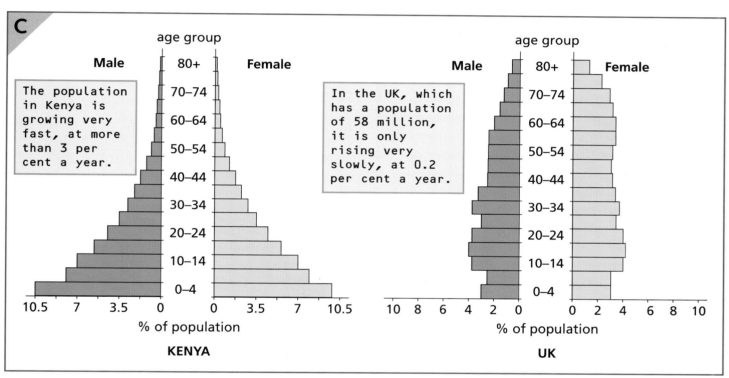

The population in Kenya is growing very fast, at more than 3 per cent a year.

In the UK, which has a population of 58 million, it is only rising very slowly, at 0.2 per cent a year.

Population pyramids for Kenya and for the UK

STEP 1

1 Use the figures in table **B** to draw a graph showing the rise in Kenya's population between 1960 and 2020.
2 Using actual figures, describe the change in population:
   a from 1960 to 1980
   b from 1980 to 2000
   c from 1960 to 2000.
   What do these figures tell you about the rate of increase?

3 Suggest what Kenya's total population might be by the year 2020.
4 Look at the population pyramids in diagram **C**.
   a Describe three differences between the population structures of Kenya and Britain. Refer to 'People under 15', 'People aged 15–65' and 'People over 65'.
   b How much faster is Kenya's population growing than the UK's population?

http://www.unicef.org/statis

 • describing population changes • • drawing a graph • calculating data • **111**

Population patterns

Life in rural Kenya

Life in urban Kenya

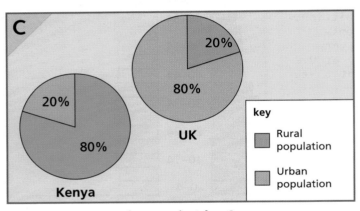

Kenya – a rural population?

Population **distribution** is the way people are spread across a country. Sparsely populated areas have very few people per square kilometre (km²). Densely populated areas have many people per square kilometre. The pattern of population in a country is related to its resources. Where there are resources there are likely to be more people. Most people in Kenya work in agriculture (figure **C**). Compare the maps **D** and **E**, and look back to map **D** on page 105.

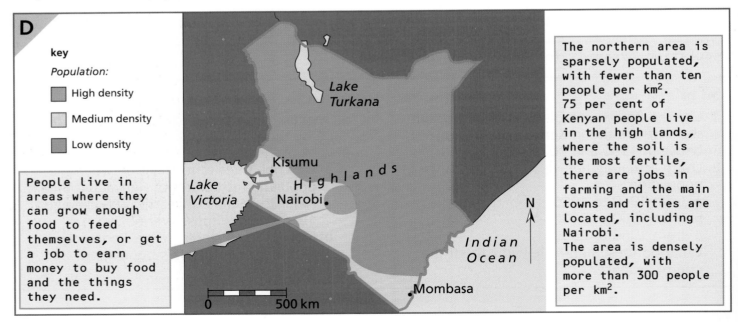

D

key

Population:

High density

Medium density

Low density

People live in areas where they can grow enough food to feed themselves, or get a job to earn money to buy food and the things they need.

Lake Turkana

Kisumu

Lake Victoria

Nairobi

H i g h l a n d s

N

Indian Ocean

Mombasa

0   500 km

The northern area is sparsely populated, with fewer than ten people per km². 75 per cent of Kenyan people live in the high lands, where the soil is the most fertile, there are jobs in farming and the main towns and cities are located, including Nairobi. The area is densely populated, with more than 300 people per km².

Population in Kenya

Population change: people on the move

Many people are moving from the rural areas (photograph **A** on page 112) into the towns and cities (photograph **B** on page 112) for several reasons. The size of the population is increasing (see table **B** on page 110) and there is not enough good farmland to support the growing number of people. Young people especially young men, move to the towns to look for work. In some places, especially in game reserves and national parks, local people are being forced to leave their own land, so that it can be developed for tourism or agriculture. Communities are being destroyed (see diagram **C** on page 107).

STEP 2

1 To calculate population density (people per km^2) divide the total population by the total area: $\dfrac{\text{total population}}{\text{total area}}$

	Kenya	UK
Total population (millions)	28	58
Total area (km^2)	580,370	244,755

Use a calculator to find the average population densities of Kenya and the UK.

Write a sentence describing the difference between the two countries.

2 Look at maps **D** and **E**.
  a Where are the most important farming areas, the most densely populated areas and the most sparsely populated areas?
  b Explain the links between your answers.
3 Your family is moving from the Kenyan high lands to Mombasa. What differences will there be in your life? (Think of scenery, climate, people, jobs.)

E

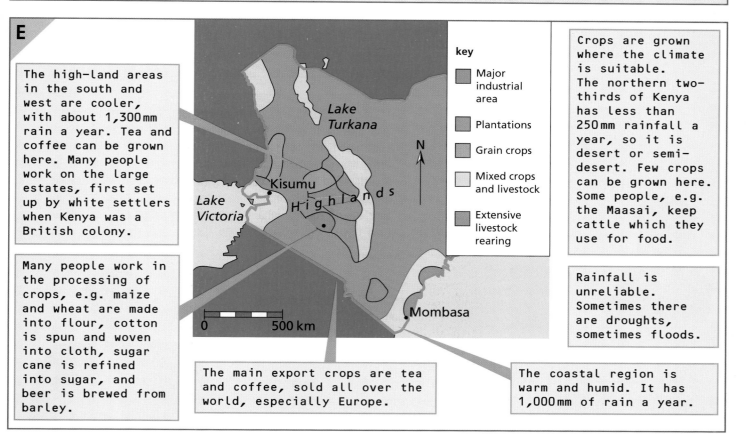

The high-land areas in the south and west are cooler, with about 1,300 mm rain a year. Tea and coffee can be grown here. Many people work on the large estates, first set up by white settlers when Kenya was a British colony.

Many people work in the processing of crops, e.g. maize and wheat are made into flour, cotton is spun and woven into cloth, sugar cane is refined into sugar, and beer is brewed from barley.

key
- Major industrial area
- Plantations
- Grain crops
- Mixed crops and livestock
- Extensive livestock rearing

Crops are grown where the climate is suitable. The northern two-thirds of Kenya has less than 250 mm rainfall a year, so it is desert or semi-desert. Few crops can be grown here. Some people, e.g. the Maasai, keep cattle which they use for food.

Rainfall is unreliable. Sometimes there are droughts, sometimes floods.

The main export crops are tea and coffee, sold all over the world, especially Europe.

The coastal region is warm and humid. It has 1,000 mm of rain a year.

Lake Turkana
Lake Victoria
Kisumu
Highlands
Mombasa
N
0   500 km

Agriculture and industry in Kenya

A

The total population is not the main problem in Kenya.

The population density is not the main problem in Kenya.

Then what is the main problem with population in Kenya?

B

The balance of resources

Kenya's total population is only about half that of the UK. But the population is made up of a large number of young people who are likely to have families, and as a result the total population will increase very rapidly. Great pressure will be put on Kenya's resources because there will be more and more people needing food to eat, houses to live in, wood for fires, water to drink, and schools and hospitals.

Resources are things like the soil, water, natural vegetation (plants), animals, beautiful scenery, minerals, crops – and the people themselves.

It is this *balance* between population and resources that is the key to the future. This is what will decide the standard of living of most people in Kenya. Getting the balance right between population and resources depends on answering several questions correctly, and dealing with them in the right way.

C

Is there enough fertile land to grow all the food that people need?

Question 1

Question 2

Is there enough industry to provide the jobs that people need?

There is a shortage of good-quality land for the small farmers who provide food for their families. Much of the country is semi-desert and the rainfall is very unreliable. At the end of 1998, heavy rains caused floods in some areas. The Agriculture Minister said that 'the combination of heavy rains, floods and droughts will mean major shortages of food'. There is also a shortage of suitable land to grow fodder crops to feed animals. Land is sometimes overused and then it loses its fertility.

Answer 1

Although there are some industries in Kenya, e.g. food processing and making cement, there are not enough jobs for everyone. Lots of people have to share jobs, or do part-time work for very low pay. Modern factories often use machinery rather than employ large numbers of people.

Answer 2

C

Will there be enough goods for export to earn the money that the country needs to build roads, schools, and hospitals?

Question 3

Question 4

Will Kenya be able to pay off its debts? In the past it has borrowed money from the richer countries (MEDCs), but these loans have to be paid back, don't they?

A country earns money by selling its raw materials (like salt), manufactured goods (like processed food) and services (like tourism). The total amount of money earned by a country is called its gross domestic product (GDP). The GDP for Kenya in the late 1980s was US¢ 380 per person, but recent estimates give a figure of less than US¢ 300. The GDP is going down, not up! This means there is not enough money coming into Kenya to buy all the things like roads, water and sewerage systems, hospitals and schools that the government would like to build.

Answer 3

Answer 4

Debt is a big problem in many LEDCs. Kenya did borrow large sums of money to help set up industries and build roads and offices. Now it has to pay off the debts, and also pay interest on the loans.

D

Overgrazed grass on Kikuyu farm, Kenya

STEP 3

1 Look at Factfile **B**.
  a One 'resource' is land (to grow food). Make a list of other resources, and explain how each one is useful. Remember to include 'people' on your list.
  b As the population increases, what will happen to the resources? Explain why this is a problem for Kenya.
2 Look at photograph **D**. What does the scene in **D** show? Why is this a problem for the people who live in that area?

Extension/Discussion

Many people think that debts owed by LEDCs to MEDCs should be 'written off' (cancelled). Find out more about the action that is being taken to try to cancel this 'Third World Debt'. Do you think the debts should be cancelled? Explain your answer.

Using the Internet

See www.oxfam.org.uk

It's a fair trade?

Many people in Kenya are farmers or work to process the goods produced by the farmers: maize and wheat are made into flour, cotton is spun and woven into cloth, sugar cane is refined, coffee and tea are dried and packaged. As in many other LEDCs, when these goods are exported, they are sold at quite low prices. Exports of raw materials like food products and minerals do not go up much in price, but prices for manufactured goods like machinery, vehicles and chemicals are often high. Most of Kenya's exports are raw materials, and it has to import most of the manufactured goods it needs. This means that it has to pay a lot for the goods it imports, but does not earn so much money from the goods it exports (diagram **A**).

A

price for exports

cost of manufactured goods

Kenya's balance of trade

The problem

Many farmers in LEDCs sell their goods to large companies at low prices. These companies are usually based in an MEDC. They are often called multinationals, or transnationals and are very powerful. They pay a lower price for goods, and then sell them at a higher price to make a profit.

The answer

Fair trading organisations like Cafédirect® and Teadirect® (advertisement **B**) try to make sure that farmers in LEDCs receive more of the money that we spend on their products. We have to pay more, but that money goes to the farmer, and helps to buy more seed, new machinery and fertilisers. The community can also afford to invest in healthcare and education.

Fair trading

B PUT THE GROWERS FIRST

cafédirect & teadirect

STEP 4

1 How will the success of fair trading organisations help to slow the movement of people from rural areas in Kenya?
2 Suggest some other products in Kenya that could be supported by fair trading organisations.

Extension

Write a paragraph for a publicity leaflet to encourage people to support fair trading. How will you persuade them to pay more for products?

Homework

• Check the cost of a fair trade product when you next go to the shops. Does it cost more than the brand your family usually uses? How much more?
• Other fair trading organisations help people who make traditional crafts to get a fair price. Find out details of these, and create a classroom display of what you find. (e.g. Oxfam and Traidcraft.)

THINKING THROUGH YOUR ENQUIRY

Your task is to write an essay called 'Describe and explain the patterns of population in Kenya', for a geography examination or for homework.

Before you write an essay, it is a good idea to make an outline plan. Copy the plan below into your exercise book, and then add notes to your plan in answer to each question.

Now write your essay using these questions and your answers to them. Set out your essay in a series of paragraphs to match your notes – see the writing frame below. Try to include some examples and figures, using material in this unit and from your own research.

Outline plan

1 Kenya.
- Location – where is it?
- Landscape – what is it like?
- People – what are the people like?

2 Pattern.
- Which areas have most people living in them?
- Which areas have few people living in them?
- Where are the main towns and cities (include a map)?

3 Reasons for pattern.
- Why do people live in certain areas?

4 Changes.
- Where are people moving from, and where to?
- Can we explain the changes?
- How might the percentage of people in towns change?

Writing frame

Paragraph 1: Brief introduction to Kenya.
Kenya is a country in …
It is made up of different landscapes, such as …
The people are …

Paragraph 2: Describe the population pattern.
Some areas such as … are densely populated and have many people per square kilometre. Other areas such as … are sparsely populated. Large numbers of people live in the main towns and cities, such as …

Paragraph 3: Explain the pattern.
Many factors affect the population density.
These include …
Large numbers of people are found in some areas, such as …
Some areas, such as … , have very few people because …

Paragraph 4: Conclusions and predictions.
The population in Kenya is likely to … in the future.
The percentage of young people is already …
The population in rural areas is likely to … unless …
The population of towns and cities is likely to …
A large population will cause problems in the future, such as …

Extension

Brainstorm/discuss in groups what effect a rapid rise in population and large numbers of young people will have in the future, in countries like Kenya, on:

- cities
- hospitals
- schools
- food supply
- transport
- landscape.

http://www.oxfam.org.uk/atwork/where/africa/kenya.htm
http://www.cafedirect.co.uk

 • writing publicity material • writing an essay • brainstorming •

6c Kenya
• How does tourism affect Kenya? •

People's homeland – or the greatest game show on Earth?

• Why is tourism so important to Kenya?

• How does it affect people and the environment?

Tourism is one of the fastest-growing industries in the world. People in richer countries now travel further and more often to take holidays. Kenya has many attractions for tourists.

On safari in Kenya

Tourist lodges, Kenya

Maasai people dressed up for the tourists

YOUR ENQUIRY

In this enquiry you will:
• understand the effects of the tourist industry on the environment
• look at the different ways of managing the environment
• consider how to develop Kenya's tourist industry without damaging the local people's environment

• understand that people's actions may have unintended environmental consequences, and that change sometimes leads to conflicting views on the environment.

At the end of the enquiry you will write a report with the title 'Ecotourism: sustainable development in action'.

• drawing a climate graph • comparing countries' weather • research •

On safari ... and on the tropical coast

D

Welcome to Mombasa

Enjoy:
- Beautiful beaches
- exciting water sports
- comfortable hotels
- spectacular coral reefs

E

Tourism in Kenya

- Number of tourists:

1960	150,000
1990	900,000

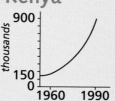

- Money earned from tourism:

1960	US$ 51.8 million
1990	US$ 467 million

- Percentage of Kenya's income from tourism:

1960	6%
1990	20%

(This is equal to half Kenya's total exports, and equal to nearly all the coffee and tea that the country exports.)

- Tourism employs well over 40,000 people directly, and many more in jobs connected with tourism.

F

Mombasa's climate

	Jan.	Feb.	Mar.	Apr.	May	Jun.	Jul.	Aug.	Sep.	Oct.	Nov.	Dec.
Max. daily temperature (°C)	32	32	33	31	29	29	28	28	29	30	31	32
Av. monthly rainfall (mm)	17	10	30	108	149	54	34	47	46	62	66	32
Sunshine (av. hours/day)	8	9	9	8	6	8	7	8	9	9	9	9

STEP 1

1 Use the figures in table **F** to draw a graph showing temperature and rainfall in Mombasa.
2 **a** Use an atlas to find temperature and rainfall figures for the UK or your local area.
  b How does Kenya's weather compare with the weather in the UK or your local area?
3 Why would Kenya's weather attract tourists from Europe in the period November–March?
4 Suggest three reasons other than climate why people might go on holiday to Kenya.

5 How could the numbers of tourists and vehicles affect animals in the game parks?

Homework/Research
- Check today's weather for Mombasa on the Internet and compare it with the weather in your own local area.
- Using travel brochures and/or the Internet sites, plan *either* a safari holiday *or* a beach holiday in Kenya.

http://www.gorp.com/guerba
http://www.kenyaweb.com/tourism/parks

Tourism – the benefits and the costs

Many tourists come from the richer, more economically developed countries (MEDCs) in 'the north' (e.g. Europe and North America) and travel to the less economically developed countries (LEDCs) in 'the south' (e.g. Africa and South America). Tourism is one way in which people in the south are linked to people in the north. Tourism brings people to Kenya – and it brings many other things too.

Tourism has advantages (benefits) and disadvantages (costs) to a country like Kenya.

A

Tourism is good for our country and the people. It can encourage the building of new roads and better communications, and provides the money to build schools and hospitals.

Government official

Tourism creates many new jobs in hotels, restaurants and services. It can develop local people's business skills and give them new ideas. Tourism sometimes creates a demand for local food from local farmers, who can then sell more crops.

Business woman

By creating national parks or game reserves which tourists like to visit, we also encourage people to protect the environment. Tourism can provide money to help keep local customs and culture alive. It creates a market for local crafts and provides jobs in the national parks and game reserves for guides.

Game warden

Advantages of tourism

B

Government minister

In order to protect our land, Kenya has set up national parks and game reserves. In these areas, conservation comes first. We need to look after our precious environment – to save it from overgrazing by farmers, and to protect the wildlife from poachers who try to kill some animals, for example elephants for their ivory. Local people can now make more money from tourists than they do from farming. It is in their own interest to help conserve our game parks.

Caring for a precious environment

C

There is no community that has suffered from a lack of basic human rights as the Maasai people. We cannot live in the national parks, and some of us have been forced off our own land. We are no longer allowed to graze our cattle in national parks or game reserves. We are seen as a tourist attraction — everyone expects us to be uneducated cattle herders with a quaint way of life and a colourful traditional dress. We want to keep our dignity, but we are treated with little respect.

Maasai concern about tourism

D

Forbidden vehicle tracks seen from a hot-air balloon

I'm concerned about some of the developments in tourism.
Safari minibuses often drive too close to animals and disturb them. They also make the dirt tracks wider, and cause soil erosion.
Hot-air balloons are used by some companies, and these too can disturb the wildlife.
In some areas, wild animals like elephants often move outside the reserves. They may destroy farmers' crops — it's not easy to keep wild animals under control.

A concerned tourist

E

Along the coast, environments are being damaged.
Coral reefs are exposed at low tide. Some tourists break off bits as souvenirs, and boat anchors can damage the coral too. The tiny animals that form coral reefs are being killed by pollution and disturbance.
The sea and beaches are polluted by waste from hotels. Local fishermen are then affected because the fish die.
Valuable farmland, trees and plants along the coast are being cut down to make way for new roads and hotels, so destroying the natural habitats that are homes for wild animals and plants.
Large amounts of water are needed for tourists in the hotels, when there is often little to spare.

An environmentalist

Litter pollution around coast near hotel

STEP 2

1 Look carefully at the different points made in the resources on pages 120 and 121. Then make a large copy of the following table, and put each of the points into the correct box on your table.

	Benefits	Costs
Environmental	. . . .	disturbing wildlife
Economic	jobs	. . . .
Social	jobs	. . . .

2 Who do you think benefits most from tourism? Who benefits the least?

http://www.gorp.com/gorp/location/africa/kenya/kenyamap.htm

The way forward – ecotourism

Tourism is now vital to Kenya's economy. It brings in US$ 467 million a year. This is 20 per cent of the country's income. So it is important to protect the natural attractions so that people will continue to visit them. To do this, Kenya must develop **sustainable** **tourism**. This means using resources carefully and wisely, so that the environment is not damaged. People in the future can then enjoy the country's attractions in just the same way that we do today. How can this be done? The answer is **ecotourism**.

A   What is ecotourism?

- **Education**
  Make both tourists and local people aware, e.g. explain why visitors to an area should be limited so vegetation can be allowed to re-grow in trampled areas.
- **Resources**
  Control the use of resources (water, energy), e.g. use fewer, low-energy vehicles, recycle materials, grow organic food. Tourists should be encouraged to eat local, not imported, food – this helps the environment, and gives local people an income.
- **Traditions**
  Allow local people to continue their 'tried and tested' methods of agriculture. Encourage traditional crafts, e.g. wood carving, which allow local people to develop their skills and, with dignity, to earn a living.
- **Money**
  Caring for the environment costs money. Part of the income from tourism can be used for this. If tour companies are involved in providing money to help support the environment, they are more likely to respect the needs of the environment and local people.

B
Home for the Maasai

C
A well-constructed safari camp

STEP 3

1 In your own words, write a clear definition of 'ecotourism'.
2 Which of the following tourist activities do you think would be considered to be sustainable tourism? Explain your answers.
  - Jet-skiing at Mombasa.
  - Planting young trees in a forest area.
  - Looking at wildlife in a safari park with a local guide.
  - Buying coral in a souvenir shop.

3 Suggest at least four more ways in which a tour company could attract tourists without harming the environment.

Extension

Why do you think it is important for local people, anywhere in the world, to be able to earn a living 'with dignity'? What does that mean?

THINKING THROUGH YOUR ENQUIRY

The government of Kenya wants to encourage environment-friendly ecotourism.

You have been asked to write a report for the government of Kenya, outlining ways to promote sustainable ecotourism. This means developing tourism in the future so that it brings in money but does not harm the people or the environment.

- The tour companies are happy to change their holiday packages if they can see the benefits of doing so.
- The government will pass laws if it has to.

Work in groups for this enquiry.

'Ecotourism: sustainable development in action'

1 First role-play the discussion between the people involved in writing the report. You will need to consider the views of:

- government ministers
- tour operators (holiday companies)
- hotel owners
- local people, e.g. the Maasai people
- environmentalists.

Each person should take one role. Research your own role, using material in this unit and other sources of information, e.g. tourist offices, libraries, development agencies, websites..

Write down three or four reasons in favour of your **argument**.

2 Following the discussion, each group member should select one of the following subjects:

- coral reefs
- safari parks
- building new hotels
- the rights of local people, e.g. the Maasai.

List the problems caused or encountered by your subject.

3 As a group, put together your report using the information you gathered in (**1**) and (**2**).

a Consider some of the following issues when writing your report:
- design of hotels
- food for hotels
- water supply
- money from tourism
- protecting the wildlife
- local customs and religion
- local farmers and fishermen
- people who work in tourism.

b Include suggestions for action to increase the amount of environment-friendly tourism on offer.

Extension/Homework

Draw up a code of conduct for tourists: five ways in which tourists should act when visiting the country. This could be presented as an illustrated poster to go in holiday brochures.

Glossary

Abrasion	a type of erosion, for example where rocks carried along by glaciers wear away other rocks
Agglomeration	a large urban area where several settlements have joined together
Alps	a range of mountains in Europe. The highest peak is Mt. Blanc (French Alps)
Arête	a rugged knife-edge mountain ridge carved out by glaciers and weathering
Avalanche	a large rapid fall of ice and snow from a mountain area. A natural hazard
Brownfield site	an area of land that has been built upon and is now derelict
Channel	a groove cut into the land by flowing rivers
Col	a gap through the mountains, often carved out by ice. Also known as a pass
Colony	a country ruled over by another country
Commute	travel to work daily
Commuters	people who travel to work every day
Crevasse	a deep split in the surface of a glacier, caused by the ice stretching and cracking. They are very dangerous, especially as they often close up as the glacier moves
Deposition	the process by which material such as mud, sand or shingle builds up new land
Distribution	the way in which physical or human features (e.g. people, rainfall) are spread out
Ecotourism	tourism which does not spoil or damage the area visited
Elevation	the height above sea level
Estuary	the mouth of a river where it flows into the sea or a lake
Eye of the storm	the centre of a hurricane where it is calm
Flash flood	a flood which happens quickly
Flood	when a river overflows its banks
Footprint	the area of land needed to provide the resources for something
Front	line separating warm and cold air masses
Frost action	repeated freezing and melting of water in cracks in rocks
Function	the main purpose or activity: for a town this could be industrial, as a port, or as a holiday resort

Gabion	a large metal cage full of pebbles or rocks for protecting coastlines
Glacier	a moving 'river' of ice. They can be very wide and deep and move downhill at different speeds, often very slowly. They are very powerful
Greenfield site	an area of the countryside where building development is planned
Hamlet	a very small settlement without services
Human	feature, process or pattern connected with people
Human factors	man-made things including transport, money, markets, industry and energy
Humid	hot and wet (usually refers to climate)
Hurricane	a violent spinning storm
Hydraulic action	when water traps air in a rock, helping to break it up
Ice Age	a long period of time when parts of the world were fully covered by ice and glaciers
Impermeable	does not let water pass through
Intensity	strength
LEDC	less economically developed country – usually a poorer country
Location	where something is placed
Longshore drift	the movement of sand and shingle along a beach
Manufacturing	the making or producing of goods
Market	a place where goods and services are sold
Migration	movement of people from one place to another
Moraine	rocks, stones and other debris carried in, under or on the glacier. Different varieties include terminal moraine (in front), lateral moraine (at the sides), medial moraine (in the middle) and ground moraine (in and under)
Multi-functional	has more than one use
Pattern	regular, repeated arrangement of physical or human features
Peninsula	an area of land surrounded on three sides by water
Physical	created by natural forces

Glossary

Physical factors	natural things including climate, relief, vegetation and water
Plucking	another type of wearing away by glaciers, when they 'pluck' or break off any rocks and boulders which get in their way
Pollution	damage to the natural world caused by humans
Population explosion	rapid rise in the population of an area/country
Population structure	the make-up of the population by age and gender
Processes	changes caused by physical or human forces, e.g. erosion
Quality of environment	the measure of how good a place is to live in
Raw materials	natural and man-made materials used to make goods
Redevelopment	where old buildings and land are replaced by new buildings
Regime	a river's annual discharge pattern
Relief	the shape of the land, i.e. highland or lowland
Remote	distant and often isolated
Resources	things which provide for people's needs – e.g. food, water, minerals, power supply
Rivers	bodies of water which flow over the landscape
Route centre	a place where transport routes join or merge. These might include ferry routes, railway lines, roads, canals and even paths
Rural settlements	small settlements built in the countryside, i.e. villages and hamlets
Saturated soil	waterlogged soil which can hold no more liquid
Savanna	area of tall grasses with occasional trees
Secondary sector	industries which manufacture or produce goods

Services	facilities like cinemas, doctors, banks, shops and clubs, that are found in settlements and used by people who live there
Settlement	a place where people live
Settlement hierarchy	the ordering or ranking of settlements based upon the number of people living in them or the services they offer
Situation	where a settlement is built in relation to other settlements and lines of communication
Snout	the front edge of a glacier
Subsistence farming	growing food just to feed the farmer's family
Sustainable development	using resources in a way that conserves them for the future
Sustainable tourism	tourism which does not destroy the environment
Tombolo	piece of land joining the mainland to an island
Track	the path taken by a hurricane
Traffic congestion	when traffic is slowed as a result of large numbers of vehicles
Transportation	the movement of material, e.g. mud, sand or shingle, from one place to another
Tropical	relating to the area between the tropics of Capricorn and Cancer
Urbanisation	growth of settlements into larger towns and cities
Urban settlements	towns and cities
Village	a small rural settlement
Water vapour	water in the form of gas

Map keys

Map key for pages 7 and 9

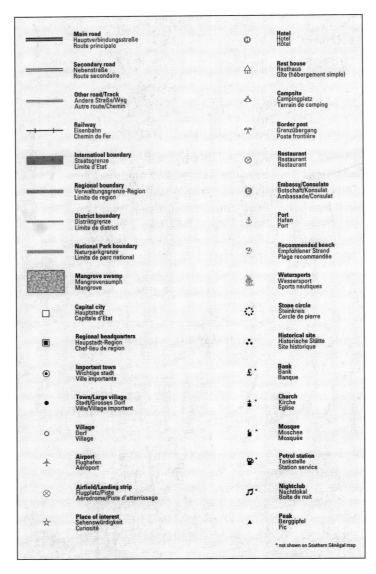

	Main road Hauptverbindungsstraße Route principale		**Hotel** Hotel Hôtel
	Secondary road Nebenstraße Route secondaire		**Rest house** Rasthaus Gîte (hébergement simple)
	Other road/Track Andere Straße/Weg Autre route/Chemin		**Campsite** Campingplatz Terrain de camping
	Railway Eisenbahn Chemin de Fer		**Border post** Grenzübergang Poste frontière
	International boundary Staatsgrenze Limite d'Etat		**Restaurant** Restaurant Restaurant
	Regional boundary Verwaltungsgrenze-Region Limite de region		**Embassy/Consulate** Botschaft/Konsulat Ambassade/Consulat
	District boundary Distriktgrenze Limite de district		**Port** Hafen Port
	National Park boundary Naturparkgrenze Limite de parc national		**Recommended beach** Empfohlener Strand Plage recommandée
	Mangrove swamp Mangrovensumpf Mangrove		**Watersports** Wassersport Sports nautiques
	Capital city Hauptstadt Capitale d'Etat		**Stone circle** Steinkreis Cercle de pierre
	Regional headquarters Hauptstadt-Region Chef-lieu de region		**Historical site** Historische Stätte Site historique
	Important town Wichtige stadt Ville importante		**Bank** Bank Banque
	Town/Large village Stadt/Grosses Dorf Ville/Village important		**Church** Kirche Eglise
	Village Dorf Village		**Mosque** Moschee Mosquée
	Airport Flughafen Aéroport		**Petrol station** Tankstelle Station service
	Airfield/Landing strip Flugplatz/Piste Aérodrome/Piste d'atterrissage		**Nightclub** Nachtlokal Boîte de nuit
	Place of interest Sehenswürdigkeit Curiosité		**Peak** Berggipfel Pic

* not shown on Southern Sénégal map

1:25 000 map key for pages 13 and 66

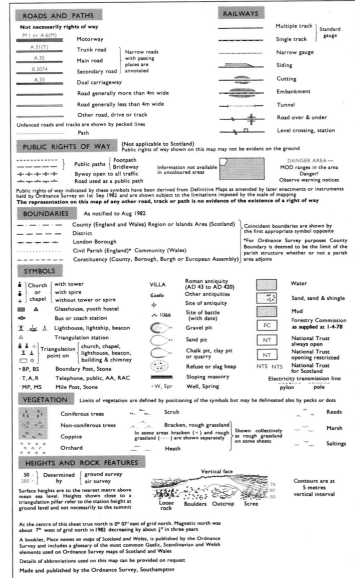

ROADS AND PATHS

Not necessarily rights of way

M I or A 6(M)	Motorway	
A 31(T)	Trunk road	Narrow roads with passing places are annotated
A 35	Main road	
B 3074	Secondary road	
A 35	Dual carriageway	
	Road generally more than 4m wide	
	Road generally less than 4m wide	
	Other road, drive or track	

Unfenced roads and tracks are shown by pecked lines

········· Path

RAILWAYS

	Multiple track ⎫ Standard
	Single track ⎬ gauge
	Narrow gauge
	Siding
	Cutting
	Embankment
	Tunnel
	Road over & under
	Level crossing, station

PUBLIC RIGHTS OF WAY (Not applicable to Scotland)
Public rights of way shown on this map may not be evident on the ground

Public paths ⎰ Footpath ⎱ Bridleway
+++++ Byway open to all traffic
Road used as a public path

Information not available in uncoloured areas

DANGER AREA— MOD ranges in the area Danger! Observe warning notices

Public rights of way indicated by these symbols have been derived from Definitive Maps as amended by later enactments or instruments held by Ordnance Survey on 1st Sep 1982 and are shown subject to the limitations imposed by the scale of mapping
The representation on this map of any other road, track or path is no evidence of the existence of a right of way

BOUNDARIES As notified to Aug 1982

	County (England and Wales) Region or Islands Area (Scotland)	Coincident boundaries are shown by the first appropriate symbol opposite
	District	
	London Borough	*For Ordnance Survey purposes County Boundary is deemed to be the limit of the parish structure whether or not a parish area adjoins
	Civil Parish (England)* Community (Wales)	
	Constituency (County, Borough, Burgh or European Assembly)	

SYMBOLS

Church or chapel	with tower with spire without tower or spire	VILLA	Roman antiquity (AD 43 to AD 420)	Water
	Glasshouse, youth hostel	Castle	Other antiquities	Sand, sand & shingle
	Bus or coach station		Site of antiquity	Mud
	Lighthouse, lightship, beacon	⚔ 1066	Site of battle (with date)	FC Forestry Commission as supplied at 1-4-78
	Triangulation station		Gravel pit	NT National Trust always open
Triangulation point on	church, chapel, lighthouse, beacon, building & chimney		Sand pit	NT National Trust opening restricted
° BP, BS	Boundary Post, Stone		Chalk pit, clay pit or quarry	NTS NTS National Trust for Scotland
· T, A, R	Telephone, public, AA, RAC		Refuse or slag heap	Electricity transmission line pylon pole
· MP, MS	Mile Post, Stone		Sloping masonry	
		° W, Spr	Well, Spring	

VEGETATION Limits of vegetation are defined by positioning of the symbols but may be delineated also by pecks or dots

	Coniferous trees		Scrub	Reeds
	Non-coniferous trees		Bracken, rough grassland	Marsh
	Coppice	In some areas bracken (ˇ) and rough grassland (······) are shown separately	Shown collectively as rough grassland on some sheets	
	Orchard			Saltings
	Heath			

HEIGHTS AND ROCK FEATURES

50 · 285 ·	Determined by	ground survey air survey

Surface heights are to the nearest metre above mean sea level. Heights shown close to a triangulation pillar refer to the station height at ground level and not necessarily to the summit

Vertical face

Loose rock   Boulders   Outcrop   Scree

Contours are at 5 metres vertical interval

At the centre of this sheet true north is 0° 07' east of grid north. Magnetic north was about 7° west of grid north in 1982 decreasing by about ½° in three years

A booklet, *Place names on maps of Scotland and Wales*, is published by the Ordnance Survey and includes a glossary of the most common Gaelic, Scandinavian and Welsh elements used on Ordnance Survey maps of Scotland and Wales

Details of abbreviations used on this map can be provided on request

Made and published by the Ordnance Survey, Southampton

1:50 000 map key for page 38

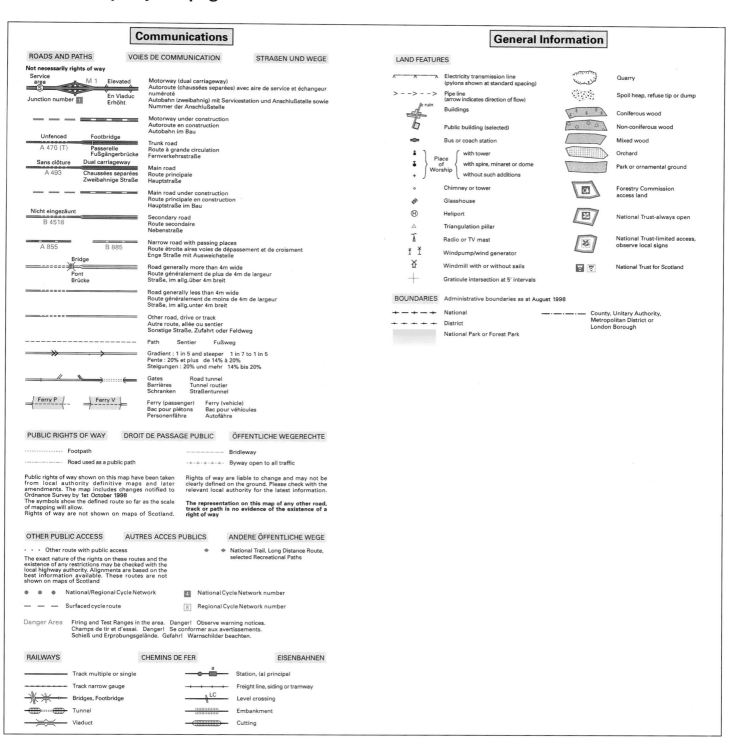

Communications

ROADS AND PATHS   **VOIES DE COMMUNICATION**   **STRAßEN UND WEGE**

Not necessarily rights of way

Service area (S)   M 1   Elevated   En Viaduc   Erhöht   Junction number 1
Motorway (dual carriageway)
Autoroute (chaussées separées) avec aire de service et échangeur numéroté
Autobahn (zweibahnig) mit Servicestation und Anschlußstelle sowie Nummer der Anschlußstelle

Motorway under construction
Autoroute en construction
Autobahn im Bau

Unfenced   Footbridge   A 470 (T)   Passerelle Fußgängerbrücke   Sans clôture   Dual carriageway   A 493   Chaussées separées Zweibahnige Straße
Trunk road
Route à grande circulation
Fernverkehrsstraße

Main road
Route principale
Hauptstraße

Nicht eingezäunt   B 4518
Main road under construction
Route principale en construction
Hauptstraße im Bau

A 855   B 885
Secondary road
Route secondaire
Nebenstraße

Narrow road with passing places
Route étroite aires voies de dépassement et de croisment
Enge Straße mit Ausweichstelle

Bridge   Pont   Brücke
Road generally more than 4m wide
Route généralement de plus de 4m de largeur
Straße, im allg.über 4m breit

Road generally less than 4m wide
Route généralement de moins de 4m de largeur
Straße, im allg.unter 4m breit

Other road, drive or track
Autre route, allée ou sentier
Sonstige Straße, Zufahrt oder Feldweg

Path   Sentier   Fußweg

Gradient : 1 in 5 and steeper   1 in 7 to 1 in 5
Pente : 20% et plus   de 14% à 20%
Steigungen : 20% und mehr   14% bis 20%

Gates   Road tunnel
Barrières   Tunnel routier
Schranken   Straßentunnel

Ferry P   Ferry V
Ferry (passenger)   Ferry (vehicle)
Bac pour piétons   Bac pour véhicules
Personenfähre   Autofähre

PUBLIC RIGHTS OF WAY   **DROIT DE PASSAGE PUBLIC**   **ÖFFENTLICHE WEGERECHTE**

.... Footpath
·—·—·—·— Road used as a public path

‒ ‒ ‒ ‒ ‒ ‒ Bridleway
·+·+·+·+· Byway open to all traffic

Public rights of way shown on this map have been taken from local authority definitive maps and later amendments. The map includes changes notified to Ordnance Survey by 1st October 1998
The symbols show the defined route so far as the scale of mapping will allow.
Rights of way are not shown on maps of Scotland.

Rights of way are liable to change and may not be clearly defined on the ground. Please check with the relevant local authority for the latest information.

The representation on this map of any other road, track or path is no evidence of the existence of a right of way

OTHER PUBLIC ACCESS   **AUTRES ACCES PUBLICS**   **ANDERE ÖFFENTLICHE WEGE**

· · · Other route with public access
The exact nature of the rights on these routes and the existence of any restrictions may be checked with the local highway authority. Alignments are based on the best information available. These routes are not shown on maps of Scotland

◆ ◆ National Trail, Long Distance Route, selected Recreational Paths

● ● ● National/Regional Cycle Network
— — Surfaced cycle route

4 National Cycle Network number
8 Regional Cycle Network number

Danger Area   Firing and Test Ranges in the area. Danger! Observe warning notices.
Champs de tir et d'essai. Danger! Se conformer aux avertissements.
Schieß und Erprobungsgelände. Gefahr! Warnschilder beachten.

RAILWAYS   **CHEMINS DE FER**   **EISENBAHNEN**

Track multiple or single   a   Station, (a) principal
Track narrow gauge   Freight line, siding or tramway
Bridges, Footbridge   LC   Level crossing
Tunnel   Embankment
Viaduct   Cutting

General Information

LAND FEATURES

Electricity transmission line (pylons shown at standard spacing)
Pipe line (arrow indicates direction of flow)
to ruin   Buildings
Public building (selected)
Bus or coach station
Place of Worship { with tower / with spire, minaret or dome / without such additions }
Chimney or tower
Glasshouse
Heliport
Triangulation pillar
Radio or TV mast
Windpump/wind generator
Windmill with or without sails
Graticule intersection at 5' intervals

Quarry
Spoil heap, refuse tip or dump
Coniferous wood
Non-coniferous wood
Mixed wood
Orchard
Park or ornamental ground
Forestry Commission access land
National Trust-always open
National Trust-limited access, observe local signs
National Trust for Scotland

BOUNDARIES   Administrative boundaries as at August 1998

+ — + — + — National
+ — + — + — District
National Park or Forest Park

—·—·—·— County, Unitary Authority, Metropolitan District or London Borough

PEARSON EDUCATION LIMITED
Edinburgh Gate, Harlow, Essex, CM20 2JE, England
and Associated companies throughout the World.

First published 2000
© Pearson Education Limited 2000

The rights of Mike Hillary, Julie Mickleburgh and Jeff Stanfield
to be identified as the authors of this Work have been asserted
by them in accordance with the Copyright, Designs and
Patents Act of 1988.

Printed in China
GCC/02
ISBN 0 582 40085 6

Acknowledgements

We are grateful to the following for permission to reproduce
photographs:

Bedfordshire on Sunday (Local Sunday Newspapers Ltd) pages 44, 48
bottom; cafédirect® & teadirect® page 116 middle; Colorific pages 27
top left (Alon Reininger/Contact), 67 middle left (Patrick Ward);
Ecoscene/Harwood pages 75 bottom left, 104 top right (Gryniewicz);
Environmental Images page 121 bottom left (Stephen Coyne);
Explorer pages 85 top right (H Veiller), 90 bottom right (Petit Jean),
92 bottom left (P Lorne), 95 middle right (A Kubacsi), 101 middle
right (S Cordier); Mike Hillary pages 8, 10, 20 top, 22, 68, 78, 80, 81;
Image Bank page 85 bottom left (A Choisnet); Images of Africa pages
104 middle right, 106 and 112 top left (Charlotte Thege), 110, 115
middle left, 118 top right, 120 bottom right and 122 top right and
middle right (David Keith Jones), 121 top left (Carla Signorini Jones);
Independent Picture Syndication page 18 (Peter Macdiarmid);
Magnum page 108 bottom left (Steele-Perkins); Marco Polo page 85
top left (F Bouillot); Julie Mickleburgh pages 30 middle right and
bottom, 37, 40, 41, 48 top, 95 top; 'PA' News pages 28 top right and
middle right, 58 top; Panos Pictures pages 108 top right and bottom
right, 112 top right (Marc Schlossman); Pictor International pages 5
right, 15 top, 58 bottom left, 108 top left; Popperfoto pages 61 middle
right, 62 top right; Rex Features pages 19, 27 top right, 28 bottom
right, 90 top left; Robert Harding pages 74 top left, 76 top right (C
Bowman), 93 (P Wysocki); Skyscan Photolibrary pages 12, 16 bottom
left and 31 middle right (Willliam Cross), 16 top right, 24 main
middle left (Pitkin Unichrome Ltd), 70 middle (B Croxford); Jeff
Stanfield pages 84, 86, 87, 88, 89, 95 bottom left, 98, 99 and 101 left;
Still Pictures pages 20 middle left (Hellier Mason), 20 bottom left
(Adrian Arbib), 36 (Nick Cobbing), 104 middle left (M & C Denis-
Huot), 118 middle right (Muriel Nicolotti); Stone Ltd pages 4 right
(D E Cox), 24 main top right and 27 middle centre (Chad Ehlers), 24
insert top right (Christopher Bissell), 27 bottom left (Robert Yager),
30 top right (Nicholas de Vore), 30 middle left (Robert Van der Hils);
Sunday Times (Information from Met Office) page 50 bottom left;
Sylvia Cordaiy pages 6 (Paul Kaye), 77 top right (John Farmar), 118
middle left (Johnathan Smith); Telegraph Colour Library page 4 left;
Topham PicturePoint pages 16 middle right, 50 top left, 94 top right,
119 top left; Travel Ink pages 15 middle (David Toase), 24 insert
middle left (Ted Edwards), 31 top right (Ian Booth), 85 bottom right
(Peter Devenish); Trip pages 5 left (R Powers), 64 top (M Feeney), 72
top left (B Thomas), 73 bottom right (P Terry); University of Dundee
pages 55 top left and right, 57 top.

Cover top: Environmental Image (Stephen Coyne); bottom Digital
Vision Ltd

We have been unable to trace the copyright holders of the following
and would appreciate any information which would enable us to do
so:
pages 87 left, 92 top, 100 top, 102 bottom right and 103 top.